T0225087

The Pocket Mentor for Animators

Want to work as an animator in the video games industry? Then this is the book for you. This is a friendly guide to understanding the industry that offers practical advice and guidance to prepare you for the challenge!

This book covers every step of the way, from picking universities through to your first year on the job. Outlining the whole job application process, with essential dos and don'ts, it also includes helpful animator-specific tips that might come in handy in those early years! Drawing from personal experience, along with interviews with ten incredibly talented people within the industry, this book ensures you feel supported and ready to enter the industry. From lessons learned to mistakes made, tackling imposter syndrome to finding friends, this book shares plenty for the reader to take away with them – even if that is just a bunch of things they know not to do . . .

A beginner's guide to life as an animator, this book is an invaluable resource for aspiring and seasoned pros alike.

Hollie Newsham is a lead animator working in the games industry. Her journey began with studying computer animation at the University of South Wales, where she received a first-class honours degree, landing her first job at Lucid Games within six months of graduating. She has managed to fit a lot in since 2017: she shipped her first PS5 exclusive title "Destruction AllStars", got promoted to Senior and then most recently to Lead, has directed motion capture shoots, mentored new animators and has given presentations at multiple international games conferences including Game Developers Conference (GDC) and Konsoll.

The Pocket Mentors for Games Careers Series

The Pocket Mentors for Games Careers provide the essential information and guidance needed to get and keep a job in the modern games industry. They explain in simple, clear language exactly what a beginner needs to know about education requirements, finding job opportunities, applying for roles, and acing studio interviews. Readers will learn how to navigate studio hierarchies, transfer roles and companies, work overseas, and develop their skills.

The Pocket Mentor for Video Game Writers
Anna Megill

The Pocket Mentor for Video Game Testing
Harún Ali

The Pocket Mentor for Game Community Management
Carolin Wendt

The Pocket Mentor for Animators
Hollie Newsham

For more information about this series, please visit: http://www.routledge.com/European-Animation/book-series/PMGC

The Pocket Mentor for Animators

Hollie Newsham

CRC Press
Taylor & Francis Group
Boca Raton London New York

CRC Press is an imprint of the
Taylor & Francis Group, an **informa** business

Designed cover image: Aaron Humphreys

First edition published 2025
by CRC Press
2385 NW Executive Center Drive, Suite 320, Boca Raton FL 33431

and by CRC Press
4 Park Square, Milton Park, Abingdon, Oxon, OX14 4RN

CRC Press is an imprint of Taylor & Francis Group, LLC

ISBN: 978-1-032-38397-2 (hbk)
ISBN: 978-1-032-38327-9 (pbk)
ISBN: 978-1-003-34484-1 (ebk)

DOI: 10.1201/9781003344841

Typeset in Times
by Apex CoVantage, LLC

Dedication

To my mom, dad and sister,

For always telling me I could be anything I wanted to be.

Contents

Acknowledgements

This book would not have been possible without Steven Brown's unwavering belief in me, for making me laugh when I want to cry, for bringing me chicken nuggets when I need them and picking up Luna's poops whilst I write this. For all my family and friends who believed I'd be able to write a book, thank you, for a while there I really didn't think I'd finish this! The biggest thank-you to Kristjan Zadziuk and Mike Waterworth for everything they've taught me and continue to teach me. Aaron Humphries for the insanely cool front cover! Amanda Renfroe, Christine Phelan, Ellise Collins, Lana Bachynski, Matt Lake, Max Shipley, Sankalp Sharma and Steve Bouliane for their fantastic interviews! Tom Noone for the last-minute sanity check. To Lucid Games and all the lovely people who work there. Alana and Leila, my cheerleaders! Luna, the cutest cover girl I could ask for. For my nan who kept laughing every time she asked me how the book was going . . .

In all seriousness, I am incredibly appreciative of the endless love and support that surrounds me, I really am here because of all of you.

Hello, I'm Hollie

1

1.1 WHO AM I?

My name is Hollie Newsham and I'm a Lead Animator in the games industry.

I live a cute little life living by the beach with my boyfriend, Ste, my adorable dog, Luna, and my very pretty cat, Xena.

I've always admired Animation for as long as I can remember. Disney and Dreamworks films were the main things I grew up watching, "Shrek" being my all-time favourite film. I largely based my decision on what I wanted to study at university on the basis of "it would be cool to learn how they made Shrek!"

Although I've always enjoyed playing games, the games industry was never something I'd thought much about. Which is crazy to think now because I truly love gameplay animation and game development as a whole. As a gameplay animator you truly get to embody a character, considering them in every angle of every movement, ensuring every system connects seamlessly with the last, all whilst injecting personality into everything you possibly can!

I've had the best time so far making games with some of the nicest, coolest, most talented people I've ever met – I highly recommend everyone comes and joins me!

PS. "Simpsons: Hit and Run" is the best game ever and no one can tell me otherwise!

DOI: 10.1201/9781003344841-1

1.2 WHAT IS THE POINT OF THIS BOOK?

I wanted to write this book from the point of view of someone who has been exactly where you are. I grew up having absolutely no idea what I wanted to do, I knew I liked drawing and playing on my computer and that was all that led me to applying to study animation at university! But when I told people what I wanted to do, all that everyone would say was how competitive the industry is and how I'll never get a job in it. Whilst they were correct in some respects, it *is* an extremely competitive industry that *is* very intimidating to get into – it *is not* impossible. I want this book to support you on this journey, a friendly helping hand that will guide you from school through to your first couple of years in the industry. The bottom line is . . .

This Book Is Going to Get You a Job

(Ok sure, I guess I can't promise that . . . but I'll try my best if you try your best!)

1.3 WHY LISTEN TO ME?

Don't listen to me. You can read this whole book and ignore every single word of it, I *dare you* to read the whole thing first though! Even if you only find one thing useful, one thing that you haven't seen before or thought of, that's still one more thing than before. I'll count that as a win . . .

1.3.1 A Note to the Reader

Nestled within the chapters of this book are interviews from a range of incredibly talented people who work within the games industry. I decided early on that I wouldn't specify the companies people work at, how many games they've shipped or years of experience they have. Not only because that information will quickly become outdated but because this book isn't about that. I urge you to respect each and every person you meet in this industry, not based on where they work or what they've worked on, but simply for the job they do, the experiences they've had and what you can learn from them. You'll soon find this industry is very small so above all else, be nice to people.

Wait . . . What Is Game Animation?

2

2.1 DIFFERENT TYPES OF ANIMATORS IN GAMES

"Animator" is a very loose definition of what animators are. Typically, animators are separated into three categories: gameplay, cinematic and technical. There are a lot of nuances within these roles depending on the type of studio: indie, AAA, mobile etc. but overall, these are a good way to differentiate. Sometimes your responsibilities will overlap between these categories, sometimes they won't. This will depend on the size of your team, the demands of the project and your personal goals. The great thing about this separation of responsibility is that you can concentrate on what you enjoy most and build your knowledge of a particular area.

Each of these categories of animator are commonly broken down into experience levels. This further depicts what sort of responsibilities you'll have, the types of tasks you'll receive, what will be expected of you, how much support you require etc.

These two things combined will give you a title (junior animator, senior technical animator etc.). Titles vary a lot between companies, but they all largely follow this pattern. The size of the company will typically depict how much they will break down each experience level, but you'll most commonly find junior, intermediate, senior, lead, principal, associate director and director positions.

DOI: 10.1201/9781003344841-2

2.2 THE ROLE OF A GAMEPLAY ANIMATOR

Gameplay animators use a combination of keyframe and motion capture data to crèate animations that serve gameplay. This involves working alongside designers and programmers to develop animation systems that ensure a character feels alive and connected to the intended design. There are nuanced differences to the type of animation you will need to create not only from human to creature but also from player to non-player characters (NPCs). The way an animation *feels*, and the responsiveness of user input is massively important when animating a player whereas when animating NPCs, it's more about the performance. These systems can range from a simple locomotion set to climbing to combat; each one of these systems are vividly different and encompass broadly different components yet follow similar patterns in the way of transitional and looping animations.

2.3 THE ROLE OF A CINEMATIC ANIMATOR

Cinematic animators lean more towards "movie-style" animation, creating scenes that serve narrative and storytelling. They use a mixture of keyframe and motion capture data to put purposefully staged shots together, animating to specific cameras. They work alongside the narrative team to ensure that their vision is brought to life. Cinematic animators are integral across all sectors of the entertainment industry – TV, film, games and vfx. Whether it's a cutscene in a game or a scene in a film, they are responsible for understanding what their character's emotion, motivation and purpose is both within their shot and in context to the rest of the story. Once this is established, they must convey the message of their shot through meaningful acting choices, composition and fundamentally embracing the principles of animation.

2.4 THE ROLE OF A TECHNICAL ANIMATOR

Technical animators enable animators to focus on creating animations whilst they concentrate on the correct implementation of the intended system, they provide a bridge between the creative and the technical. Their responsibilities involve the design and development of rigs and tools. Alongside this, they troubleshoot problems that arise within the pipeline, ensuring that solutions are found and improvements are made to streamline future production.

Let's Go Back to School! (Oh God I Hope Not . . .)

3

3.1 #1 – IT'S OK TO NOT KNOW WHAT YOU WANT TO DO!

You do not need to have your whole life planned out at 16.
You do not need to go to university.
You do not need to get a job in what you picked to study at university.
You do not need to have everything figured out in your 20s.
You do not need to do anything that doesn't make you happy!
It won't always be easy or simple, but the important thing is to find what you enjoy. Not everyone enjoys their job, even with "passion" jobs you aren't going to love everyday but if you're going to do something with the majority of your time, it's much more exciting when you actually like doing it!

3.1.1 It's Ok!

It's also ok if you decide animation isn't for you, or the games industry, or anything involving computers! We definitely put too much pressure on ourselves to be perfect, to not make mistakes and to not try things for fear of failure. But the paramount fact is that everybody makes mistakes, they're the best ways to learn! How will you know if something doesn't work if you

6   DOI: 10.1201/9781003344841-3

don't try it first? This is going to sound super cheesy but the only thing holding yourself back is you.

3.2 WHAT DO YOU *WANT* TO STUDY?

When you get to the part of life where you can choose what subjects to study, it can be easy to fall into the trap of picking something you don't truly want to study. You can pick subjects because your parents told you to, because your friends picked them, because they'll *look good* or because that's what you *should* pick.

Something I will always advise is, where possible, pick subjects you actually *want* to learn. Remember that you're the one who has to sit through the classes and actually learn this stuff!

Some people just really aren't drawn to anything, so people's recommendations are really helpful, that's completely understandable. Some people know from an early age what they want to do and the steps they need to take to get there – that's incredible! The only thing I would recommend here is to not restrict yourself to that one vision you have of yourself. I say this because you never know how you're going to find something, whether the reality lives up to what you imagined it to be (or be completely honest) whether you'll be any good at it!

Regardless of what you pick, give yourself room to change your mind. There's no use beating yourself up about a decision you've made and going along with something your heart isn't in. Prioritise your happy little heart! Whilst also thinking logically . . . I guess.

3.2.1 Here's Some Tips to Help . . .

3.2.1.1 Identifying Your Strengths and Weaknesses

Be honest with yourself. What subjects do you excel in? What subjects do you struggle with? Are you more creative or logical? Do you communicate better in written or spoken form? Do you prefer hands-on experience or the theory behind it?

3.2.1.2 Do Your Research

You don't need to know your exact path but it's wise to have some rough options in mind. Do a little research into universities with courses related to the subjects you're looking at picking. It's worth keeping in mind that some universities ask for specific subject qualifications and/or certain grades.

3.3 PICKING THE PERFECT UNIVERSITY

It's daunting when you first start looking at universities, there are so many! In the United Kingdom, there are over 160, let alone if you are considering studying abroad. The way to narrow this down is having some idea of what you'd like to study, then researching the best universities for those types of courses. Picking your university isn't all down to where the best course is. You need to think about university as a package; you're going to be living in this place for the next 3 years and more, so it's super important that you *actually like* the area! Make sure *all* factors come into your decision-making.

- *The Location* – of the university itself, of the student halls and of the nearest city. Look at what people say it's like to live there, past students, general residents. Do people feel safe there? Is it a nice place to walk around? How long would it take to walk into town, to walk to class, will you need to get a lot of taxis/buses/buy a bike? Is there much possibility for part-time work? (part-time jobs can be a great way not only to make money but also to develop social skills, confidence and make friends) Would you have to travel far for work?
- *The Attractions* – is there stuff to do outside of going to class? (This doesn't need to be party focused.) Are there places relevant to any of your interests/hobbies? It's so important to give yourself time to recharge and have *fun*. Are there good shops to walk around? Are there general supermarkets local? Are there restaurants and bars?
- *The Price* – if you will be needing to get local transportation, how much will that likely cost? How much is a bag of pasta? Or a box of teabags? Figure out how much your favourite meals to cook would be. How much would going out for a meal cost? Cost of living wildly varies across the country, you shouldn't necessarily let this overrule your decisions, but it needs to be considered. Managing your money is one of the biggest trials as a student!

3.4 OPEN DAYS

Take advantage of university open days. This is your chance to really scope out where you'll be spending your next three years. Ask questions!

3.4.1 Hardware/Software

Specification of the PCs available in the classroom, are they able to run comfortably? Are you expected to have a top-spec PC personally for your coursework? Is there 24-hour access to PCs in the classroom? (Not everyone has the money for an expensive setup, they should accommodate for that.) Do they support motion capture technology? If so, what sort of set up do they have? Would you have access to this opportunity freely? What programs will you be using?

3.4.2 Course Specifics

How many in-person hours a week? What sort of modules should you expect? Do you do any collaborative projects with other courses? Industry lectures? Help with internships/gap years? How much industry experience do the lecturers have? Are there any recommended reading/tutorials/talks?

3.4.3 Misc

What is the town like? Is it safe? Is there much to do? Have previous years gotten on well as a team? What have past alumni gone on to do? Is there anything you should be aware of?

3.5 WHAT SKILLS DO YOU NEED?

Animation-related courses will typically ask for an Art A-level/equivalent and sometimes a Maths too. They'll also be looking for a portfolio of work, your coursework will generally apply but it's always good to add a bit of flare.

I'd heavily recommend showing course-specific enthusiasm to this whether that's life drawing, following some animation basics tutorials (Blender is free!) and/or some game engine tutorials (Unreal Engine and Unity, also free!). Not only will that show you're ready and eager to learn but it will also give you a little grounding before beginning your course, so everything isn't as overwhelming!

A question everyone always asks me is whether you need to be able to draw to be an animator. Speaking for game animators, no, it is not *essential* to be able to draw but it definitely helps in the planning stages if you can get your idea down in some capacity. (Stick people are completely acceptable!) It's also worth noting that drawing *does* help you to understand the fundamentals of animation such as weight, balance and appeal so if you have any small interest in this skill, you will benefit from maintaining it!

3.6 DON'T FANCY UNIVERSITY?

It's not talked about enough that you do not need to go to university to achieve your dreams. It can feel like that's the only option. Of course, if you want to become a doctor or a rocket scientist, then you'll need to degree up! However, I can only assume if you've bought this book that you are probably/maybe going to become an animator! Or something mildly similar . . . And for that, there are plenty of options.

3.6.1 Online Animation Schools

Animation Mentor, iAnimate, AnimSchool, Udemy[1]

Online schools are becoming more and more prominent, especially in recent years, with the rise of remote working. This format utilises the accessibility of the greatest industry professionals from around the world in the comfort of your own home! These services come with their own challenges such as working within different time zones, potentially alongside a full-time job and lack of face-to-face interaction. These schools will require you to already own the sufficient hardware required to run their chosen software packages (depending on the software, you may need to pay for licenses – if you are not eligible for student licenses). It's important that you are self-disciplined and on top of your own time management, establishing structure can be really challenging when there is no physical accountability. You'll need money upfront, which you won't be able to supplement with student loans the same as you would with university. Whilst these courses aren't cheap, they are much more dedicated, you'll get out what you put in and you'll no doubt be taught the most up-to-date practices and workflows.

3.6.2 Self-Teaching

The other option would be to teach yourself. There are a multitude of YouTube tutorials about how to do anything and everything these days with a new one going up as I write this sentence, no doubt. Along with plenty of written resources, see *Luna's Learning Lab* for examples. The biggest thing to keep in mind when it comes to self-teaching is *don't try to skip to the end!* Don't go straight into a big cinematic animation the first time you open Maya/Blender, start simple. The "12 Principles of Animation" are the big ones to read up on first, then there's the classic bouncing ball exercise. It's important to really understand and feel confident in the fundamentals before you get overwhelmed with more complicated rigs and exercises. Simply understanding the software package is a task in itself! Get used to navigating in a 3D space, using the graph editor and setting up hot keys for tools you use a lot.

Ground your knowledge base in the whole pipeline by completing tutorials in the fields that support animation like 3D modelling and rigging. You don't have to be the world's best artist or create a super smart rig but appreciating the process before and after your section will help you. Understanding where problems can stem from, what good topology looks like, how to set up a clean skeleton and control rig, knowing the advantages and disadvantages of various workflows. These are the sorts of things you will be speaking with other departments about. Whether that's giving feedback on a rig, deciphering whether a problem in your animation is your fault or not, requesting changes to a model – you will be able to communicate these things with much more empathy and gratitude than if you had no idea what other crafts do! Never make assumptions about things you don't understand.

As I've said previously, even if you don't go into games, having a good grasp of game engines will not hurt you. Making your own game is now easier than ever, with so many free resources out there, it would be rude not to! But even if you just use it as a rendering engine, which film and TV are using more and more these days, it's an invaluable skill to have wherever you decide to go!

One thing I cannot stress enough when deciding what educational path is right for you is to try to consider this next stage of your life as a whole phase. University fees are ridiculous, they essentially are an extra tax, it's easy for that to be the focus. But the experience of moving away to a new place and figuring out how to do things on your own, with everyone around you experiencing the same thing, is something you can't really replicate. For me, the life experience, confidence, best friends and ridiculous memories I gained from those three years outweigh any reasons I had to not go.

Interview With . . . Ellise Collins | Designer[2]

I thought Ellise would be a great person to interview for this book as she began in animation before transitioning into design. It's important to note that you won't always have all the information to know exactly what you want to do, what you first choose might not be right for you and that's ok! I truly believe Ellise will be a better designer for the fact she has a breadth of experience in another field.

What made you want to work in games?

I never specifically knew I wanted to work in games, I honestly didn't know what I wanted to do. I loved games, storytelling, animation and creativity in general, but I didn't know what would fit me. I ended up going down an animation route with my degree and in doing that I gained a skill that granted me access to the games industry. This allowed me to learn so much more and led me to find the position that was truly right for me. I never knew I could be here, but I am so happy that I am.

What formal qualifications do you have, and do you think they are essential to get a job in the industry?

I have a degree in computer animation, and it definitely helped me with discovering areas I didn't think about before, but honestly, there's so much more online nowadays. Online courses, tutorials, dev-blogs, ways to connect with people that if you have the drive to learn by yourself and confidence to communicate with the dev community, it's possible to advance without one.

You have a degree in computer animation, how did you become a designer?

My first job after university was at a small indie studio making mobile games and although I was titled as an "Animator", I was much more of a general dev, getting my hands in all the sections. I loved communicating with the team and learning how and why they made things the way they did. I loved finding the solutions to things. After four years of essentially being a generalist, I then moved into a job that focused on my title as an "Animator", although I enjoyed animation, I was missing the design process and kept finding myself gravitating back to design tasks. I knew that's where I felt most at home in my thoughts. I approached my animation director and told him where my passion laid, he agreed that it was right for me to change over to design. I've been happy and thriving in my thoughts ever since.

If you could speak to past-you, what would you say?

Communicate more, be open about your lack of knowledge, express your ideas, ask questions, open up to people about what you enjoy, acknowledge when you're struggling and ask for help. It applies to so much more than just work, we're all human and everyone has struggled at some point in their life, your worth and skills aren't related to how much you know and how quickly you get there.

What advice would you give to people looking for a job?

It isn't always about the experience you have or the portfolio you show, although having a great portfolio helps. Connecting with the right people at the right time can be just as effective, going to dev meetups, conventions, connecting with people on LinkedIn and Twitter, not to communicate with them necessarily but to see the information they're putting out. There's a lot of honesty out there from devs that highlight details separate from simply creating a CV.

How did you land your first job?

I found two of my first jobs through connections. The first being a distant connection, through word of mouth, I found out about a small mobile company hiring for an internship in London. I had to live off of my savings for a few months and stay on my brother's sofa. After that, I got offered a full-time job on minimum wage (big advice here: *don't sell yourself short like I did*).

It was Hollie who pointed me towards the company.I work for now, where I got to show off my skills (but also lack of skills . . .) which led me to my true calling in Design! Eagerness to learn, willingness to contribute, respecting your team and trusting yourself, helped me get to where I am today.

Most important lesson you learned in your first year in the industry?

You don't need to rush or overwork yourself; you'll learn gradually over time through experience and from interacting with others around you. You're not expected to be at the same level or skill set as everyone around you, you'll forever be learning and improving, don't burn yourself out over fear.

What is the best quality to have to be a good game developer?

Communication really is key. Being able to discuss things within your team, understanding their different roles and where you fit within that. Always being open to learning, asking questions and taking time to appreciate other people's suggestions. Everyone is working towards the same goal; we should all strive to get the best out of each other and to combine our talents.

What would be your dream game to work on?

That's a hard one, I have so many different kinds that I'd love to work on. I'm a big fan of RPG's, hack and slash, rhythm games, surreal stories, multiple timelines and loveable characters. So, one day I'll think of a way of incorporating all that into a game.

When will you feel like you've made it?

I don't think I'll ever feel like I've "made it". I'll be happy with being respected and heard within my field, being a helpful go-to person within my team and being able to help integrate and inspire future devs.

What does success look like to you?

It's very hard to rate success, it's very individual for each person. I'd say working within a team I'm in sync with, on a game idea that I love. Producing something that's filled with personality and love from the developers, which is clear to the players. Also having the work/life balance to take breaks and take in life experiences that don't involve work.

What to do on a bad day?

Bad days are impossible to avoid, I'll be honest, I still struggle a lot with these myself. It helps to step away from your work, take a breather, go for a walk, treat yourself to a nice lemon slushie (maybe that's too specific to me . . .) and remember – work isn't your whole life, it's a small part that shouldn't always take control of your thoughts or mood.

What is the best advice you've received (so far)?

There's been a lot of encouragement that I've had along the way, especially at my current company (normally in my time of anxiety and stress):

1. Work isn't your whole life, it's just a part of your life.
2. Asking for help when you don't understand something, doesn't make you bad at your job. You'll complete a task more effectively and efficiently if you ask rather than put it all on yourself.

Final words?

Working in the games industry is supposed to be fun. It's not life or death, you're making entertainment, it should be enjoyable. The tasks you get and the pressure you put on yourself aren't worth losing sleep over. Once you start to realise that (and it is very hard to realise), you'll start to confidently shine in your creative field!

NOTES

1 I haven't used any of these services personally therefore cannot vouch for a specific one, pleasedo your own research, if you're considering this path.
2 Fun fact: Ellise and I went to university together (almost ten years ago!) and I count myself very lucky to work with her now. The real dream is working with your best friend and that's the greatest recommendation I have!

The Ultimate Game Animator's Job Application

4

It's time to put together the best damn application anyone has ever seen! That is the point of this, to be seen. You must keep in mind that your application will be going to very busy people so if you're only going to be seen for two minutes in between meetings you need to *ensure those two minutes are worth it.*

4.1 COVER LETTER

Did you know that 72.3% of people don't bother to include a cover letter? You probably didn't because I just made that up but it's almost definitely true! We rarely ever receive cover letters and when we do, they usually don't show any enthusiasm or personality. You should use every opportunity you get to make a good impression. My favourite cover letters have been ones that have done their research, have taken time to get to know what our games are and maybe share an opinion or a kind word. Fundamentally it's the ones that read like they've actually been written by a person.

4.2 CV

Your CV is an essential part of your application, although these are often much more relevant (to the interviewers) when you're applying for more senior roles, it always matters to have a clear and concise CV. The main thing

DOI: 10.1201/9781003344841-4

we'll look at is your experience and we'll clarify what your role and responsibilities were at these previous places of work. We'll also notice gaps in your history, multiple small stints at companies and larger periods where you've maybe not released anything (maybe projects were cancelled etc.). We check these things to ensure that there have been no problems in the past, no failed probations or years of coasting but we also want to hear the full story and not make presumptions. Other things we look out for in CVs are signifiers of your personality, including any hobbies or interests you have can be an opportunity to show extra qualities you could bring to the team that sets you apart from the rest.

4.2.1 Things We Don't Need to See on Your CV

- *All of your previous workplaces* – whilst it's great to see you have social skills, the ability to follow instructions, time management etc. try to narrow it down to the most recent and relevant examples. We expect junior applicants to have little to no game industry experience so don't worry about this section too much.
- *Experience level* – it's somewhat relevant to note your years of experience and what software you're familiar with but never ever say you're an "expert" of anything or rate your skill level of software on any kind of scale because it is simply a lie. People with 20+ years of experience in the industry still wouldn't describe themselves as experts of anything. Software is constantly being updated, hardware is forever advancing, new techniques are being developed every day. We never stop learning.
- *Irrelevant personal details* – your age, relationship status, personal social media handles, the results of every GCSE you took.
- *Links that don't work!!!* – send your CV to a friend or family member to proofread and test your links *before* you send it out. Fresh eyes are *always* a good idea.

4.3 SHOWREEL

Your showreel is the single most important part of your application. This is the be all and end all. We can see past no cover letter, a spelling mistake in your CV, a gap in your job history but if you have no showreel that's an instant rejection.

If we can't find your showreel, we can't do much with that. *Make sure* we can *easily* find and play your showreel.

A showreel is a cherry-picked selection of your best work. A representation of your skill set, creativity and personality. This is your chance to make a lasting impact on your viewers, you want to stand out and be memorable.

4.3.1 Guidelines

* No more than three minutes long.
* Be sensible with music choice, choose something that compliments your work.
* Start with your *best* and *favourite* clip, if your viewer only sees the first five seconds make sure it's a *killer five seconds*! (they'll probably watch the rest then too . . .)
* *Avoid excessive camera cuts* that detract from the core animation.
* Don't worry about fancy lighting and textures, they're a lovely bonus but the true focal point should be *showcasing your craft*.
* *Tailor your showreel* to what you're applying for:

  * *Gameplay animator* – shows gameplay, body mechanics, motion capture work and implementation into a game engine.
  * *Cinematic animator* – shows body and facial performance, dialogue, camera, staging and framing.
  * *Technical animator* – shows rigging, cloth dynamics, tools, pipeline improvements and scripting knowledge.

But also, *don't over tailor*. If you're an animator who also loves rigging, show that! Overlapping disciplines aren't a bad thing and often help you stand out.

* Make *every frame count* – if you're not proud of it, cut it. If you don't like it there's a high chance your viewer won't either. Don't add unnecessary bloat for the sake of making your showreel a certain length, quality over quantity. Being harsh with your edit shows a sense of discipline and an ability to distinguish what makes a presentable animation!
* *Clearly state your responsibilities*. If you show a clip from something that was a collaborative effort, label exactly what you were responsible for. It's also useful to label what is keyframe, motion capture and edited motion capture.
* Include your name and contact details (keep this up to date).

4.4 EXTRAS

Be enthusiastic about making games. Seeing some kind of understanding or at least an appreciation of how games are made and the systems that go into them will always be a plus.

Side-by-side comparisons of RAW motion capture alongside your edited motion capture, labelled where possible to explain what you did. This is a fantastic way to give us an insight into the way you work!

Showing an animation as it is in the 3D software you used and then show it working in the engine. It doesn't have to be perfect, as animators we just love seeing behind the scenes and we can appreciate the intent when you show your process.

Fundamentally, *show us* what kind of animator you want to be.

4.4.1 Make Your Own Game

Something simple, you don't need to create some massive open-world RPG all on your own, it can be anything really. A playable character whose sole purpose is to eat donuts. A can of beans that has to roll away from imminent danger. I don't know, sit down with a bunch of tutorials and see where they take you!

Sending us a link to a game *you made*, that we can play, just shows an obvious enjoyment for game development and I think that's such a cool thing to do.

Looking and Applying for Jobs *Is* Your Job

5

So, the time has come for you to find that almighty *first job in industry* everyone has been talking about. This is a super exciting time, of course, but it's also *completely terrifying*. What you must remember is that you are completely prepared for this, you deserve this and if you stay persistent you *will* find your perfect role.

5.1 THE PLAN

5.1.1 Setting the Search Parameters

There are multiple factors that need to be considered when beginning your search:

- *Location* – Are you willing to re-locate? If so, how far are you willing to move? Are there areas you would particularly like to live? Consider salary, cost of living, language, culture, even the weather! If you're thinking of moving abroad keep in mind that you will need to attain a visa. If moving isn't an option, think about commute times and figure out a radius of distance you're willing to travel.
- *Hybrid work* – Would you be willing to commute into the office for a certain number of days a week? The commute being reasonable is

DOI: 10.1201/9781003344841-5

essential for this option, but this gives you the benefit of in-person communication and building team rapport with the freedom of working in solitude at home when you need to.

- *Remote work* – Are you willing to work fully remote? Considering this as an option will open you up to more opportunities but it's important to note that fully remote work has its benefits and drawbacks. This is a massive topic that has naturally blown up since the 2020 pandemic, with many companies still figuring out what will work best for them and their employees. There are many perspectives that I recommend researching further when considering this option. I'll briefly touch on a few things that commonly come up in discussions with my colleagues, friends and family.

5.1.2 Pros of Remote Work

- *No commute* – this is especially helpful if you live far away and have to deal with rush hour traffic or busy/unreliable public transport.
- *More time for friends and family.*
- *Home comforts* – easy, stress-free environment that is completely in your control, you can upgrade your setup as you see fit.
- *Flexibility* to work around errands, kids, pets etc.
- *Control* – ability to make up your hours outside of the core working day.

5.1.3 Cons of Remote Work

- *Disconnection* – from colleagues, projects and the company. (take the opportunity to meet your team and visit the studio in person where possible)
- *Home distractions* – you can easily get caught up doing things around the house.
- *Collaboration and Communication* – in an office of people it's easier to help others and be helped yourself, to learn from general office discussions, to see what other people are up to, to offer ideas. This is a hard thing to replicate remotely.
- *Work/life balance* – the lines blur when the home is your office, it gets hard to switch off.

Ultimately this decision is down to personal preference and what opportunities are available at the time; however, my recommendation for your *first job* in the industry is to work physically in the studio. A lot of companies are looking for juniors who are willing to visit the studio on a regular basis, making yourself open to this will make you even more attractive as a candidate. Aside from it being easier to ask for help and feedback, it's the social side of it that I think is an essential part of the beginning of your career – Communication, Collaboration and Connection. Being a good animator is only the beginning of being a good game developer, it's how you interact with your team, peers and leads that will help your connection not only to your team but to the wider studio.

There will no doubt be a whole range of people with varying years of experience in the industry, with war stories about the development of games you love and games you've never heard of. Projects getting cancelled, people who went a bit crazy, the millions of hours of crunch they used to do, the way they used to apply for jobs by sending in videotapes! It's really cool to see how far the industry has come, where it still has its problems and where people see it heading. Of course, you can get this information from reading articles but it's different to hear these accounts first hand. With the opportunity to ask questions this is how you get a baseline of how you want to be treated, what you want from a studio, how you should value the work that you produce and just generally understanding the myriad of disciplines that are happening all around you. The development of your social skills and making connections with your colleagues is a fundamental part of your personal growth that is much harder to do when working remotely.

5.2 THE OBVIOUS

So, the obvious first step to finding a job as an animator is to search "animator jobs" in Google. This will give you a fair few results that every other person looking for a job as an animator will have also done. Apply for all of those jobs and we'll move on.

5.3 THE NOT-SO OBVIOUS

The next stage is social media. The greatest and worst thing to come out of modern technology! For all its faults, when used correctly this is your biggest and easiest tool that you have at your fingertips. You can instantly connect with people all around the world, with groups and communities of animators who have gone through or are going through all the same things as you. Who are often ready to help, to offer feedback on your showreel and give you tips. What are you waiting for?!

5.3.1 Social Media: Best Practices

Connect directly with people you aspire to, often these people post advertisements for jobs and post advice when applying for jobs.

There's no harm in directly contacting people but *be courteous* when doing so.

- *Do not* blanket add people with no thought, put effort into that first message to connect.
- *Do not* directly ask these people for a job.
- If they *don't* reply, leave it at that, these are busy people with their own lives.
- If they *do* reply, make sure you're sensible with what you're asking of them.
- *Do* ask for – critique on your showreel, answering specific questions about advice and their experiences.
- *Do not* ask for – feedback on several different animations, continuously sending more animations without them saying that's ok, asking generic open-ended questions that don't show any self-thought and seeming like you just want them to give you the answers, questions you could definitely answer yourself through Google, questions about the latest project they're working on.

Please treat the people you are contacting with respect; they are not obligated to do anything for you.

5.4 THE "OH I DIDN'T THINK OF THAT!"

No advert? No problem. Don't let a company not having a specific job opening on their website stop you from sending your application in. Most companies have the option to submit a speculative application, if you can't find that just email them! They may not be hiring at that moment but if you've put together a good enough application, they will keep you on file. This is where having a memorable showreel pays off. I know it's easier said than done to "be memorable" and let me be clear that I'm not saying you need to create the most astounding, earth-shattering masterpiece. It's just about thinking a little outside of the box. Be creative with your acting choices.

A frog having a cup of tea, a snail trying to fly, a chicken who is late for work.

Or even just a really tired guy walking up some stairs, an exciting lady looking at dogs – showing you can animate should be fun!

5.5 THE TRUTH

5.5.1 You Will Get Rejected

. . . and that's ok! The important thing is to not take it personally. Nobody was lying when they told you this industry is incredibly competitive. One of the hardest parts of your journey will be this first bit, getting your foot in the door.

- *Pause*. One thing I always recommend to graduates is to take a break to celebrate themselves and everything they've achieved so far! There is absolutely no rush to get that almighty first job in the industry. Take a week, a month, go on holiday, hang out with your friends and family, the industry isn't going anywhere.
- *Perseverance*. Once you're ready to begin your search, you *will get out of it what you put into it*. There are plenty of people who definitely could have "made it" if they'd just persevered. Hence, the title of this chapter – until you get a job, *getting* a job is your job.
- *Practice*. Hone the craft! Animate something that makes you happy, try a new method, and follow some tutorials. Update the weakest parts of your showreel. Take pride in keeping your skills and knowledge up to date, this will keep you in good form for when your interviews start rolling in!

You Got an Interview! Congratulations!!

6

I really do want to congratulate you here because all your hard work is paying off. You put together a great application, your showreel stood out and they want to know more!

6.1 PREPARATION AND RESEARCH

As with everything the best thing to do is be prepared.

6.1.1 Research the Company

How long has the company been established? What are their most popular games? What are their more obscure titles? Which of these games have they been the primary developer of? What genres do they specialise in? How many employees do they have? Do they have many social events within the company?

6.1.2 Look Up the Interviewers (If They've Included Their Names)

The organiser of your interview may disclose the name(s) of the people at the company who will be interviewing you. It doesn't hurt to ask in cases they

DOI: 10.1201/9781003344841-6

haven't mentioned any specifics. The reason this can be valuable to you is that you can do a little research into them. It's important to note that I don't mean stalking their social media, knowing weird specific details about them will have the opposite effect entirely. Find out what games they've worked on, how long they've worked at this company, how long they've been in the industry, their latest showreel etc. The key to this is showing a little interest, you can ask more bespoke questions and show you've put a little time into your research. It's a small gesture that goes a long way. It's also worth noting that knowing a lot about one of the interviewers and disregarding the other(s) can have a negative effect so tread carefully with this.

6.1.3 Have Questions

This should be way easier after all that research!

At the end of an interview, your interviewer will most likely ask you if you have any questions. Having a few questions ready that show your interest in the company and the position you're applying for doesn't sound unreasonable, does it? It can potentially be a bit of a red flag if you don't have *any* questions to ask. You'd be surprised at the amount of people who don't think this matters but it's actually a really great opportunity to get insight from real employees of a company you potentially want to work at!

Example Questions

- What game have you most enjoyed working on at [studio name]? and/or in your whole career?
- What made you want to work at [studio name]?
- How big is the animation department?
- Are there many opportunities to meet/socialise with the other colleagues at the studio/are there regular social events?

6.2 INSIDE THE BRAIN OF AN INTERVIEWER

With interviews for juniors, it's pretty simple. We're not looking for anything crazy (of course, if you have crazy skills, that's a plus!) I'm not speaking for all companies but in my experience, if you've made it to an interview that means your showreel/skill level is adequate enough. We'll ask you questions that will either reinforce this opinion or disprove it. What we're most looking to get out of your interview is a gauge of your attitude and personality.

6.2.1 Things We Appreciate

- Being on time
- A friendly face to greet, generally smiley and interested throughout
- Polite, open and honest answers
- Basic research into the company
- Genuine interest in animation and games
- Eagerness to learn
- A level of understanding of the fundamentals of animation
- Good fit for the team
- Something to *bring* to the team (hobbies, interests, skills and quirks)
- *If remote* – test your connection, microphone and camera beforehand
- *If remote* – be in a private space where you feel comfortable but professional, limit distractions

6.3 WHAT TO EXPECT

6.3.1 Relax and Take Time to Think When You Need It

Entering an interview will always be nerve-wracking, whether it's your first or your 21st interview. Your interviewer *should* understand that and expect the first couple of questions to be a little rocky. Hopefully, they'll ask you a couple of general questions to break the ice. No interviewer, as far as I can say, would hold some nerves and shaky words against you! Top tip: if you need some time to think of an answer, take a sip of water.

6.3.2 They *Will* Quiz Your Ability

Be ready to go through your workflow, what programs you use, how you would approach an animation, how you generate ideas . . . No one is looking to catch you out, they just want to understand how you work, what you know and what you need help with.

6.3.3 Take Notes

If you're able to, try to jot down the things they ask you and the general answers you've given. This will enable you to review what you said and how you can improve for next time.

6.3.4 First Impressions Matter

I know it's a lot of pressure but the way you come across in this interview is everything. We can see past nerves and anxieties. What we can't ignore is patronisation, arrogance and dishonesty. Be mindful of the things you say, don't disrespect other people's work, don't presume you know everything and don't belittle.

6.4 YOU DIDN'T GET THE JOB

6.4.1 It's Not the End of the World

There are so many different reasons as to why you didn't get it, it isn't necessarily anything you did or didn't do.

The first thing you can take from this is the experience, ask for feedback. If they've highlighted a specific reason you didn't get the job, take that as a golden opportunity to work on it and ensure your next interviews don't suffer the same fate.

However, more often than not, it wasn't anything that could have been helped. It's the luck of the draw who the other interviewees are and sometimes there's just another candidate that makes more sense for the role. Whether that's because of a certain obscure skill they have that would bring contrast to the team, or simply that their previous experience suits the project's needs slightly more.

The bottom line is not to lose faith and give up. *You will get a job*, sometimes it just takes a little more time.

Interview With . . . Sankalp Sharma | Animator

The best thing about San is how excited he gets about animation, games, films, food, everything really . . . It's the most wonderful thing to bring into your work and team, a genuine enthusiasm and desire to find inspiration in everything!

What made you want to work in games?

I used to play "Devil May Cry" (by Ninja Theory) a lot. I loved how the character walked and his whole personality was so cool. I used to think to myself "I want to make cool games like that!" That's when my passion for games and being in the games industry started.

What formal qualifications did you receive to become an animator? Do you think you need formal qualifications?

I was a science student when I was in India, but I always had this strong passion for making games. I did a BSc Hons in Games Design to understand how games are made. As the course went on, I found myself being drawn to animation, luckily I was able to take animation as an optional module in my third year.

A degree doesn't matter more than your skills. I think to become an animator, all you need is a good eye and your amazing work to prove that you can animate.

What do you like about being an animator?

I absolutely love being an animator as I get to give life to amazing characters and creatures that don't even exist in the real world! It lets me push my creative limits when I try to gather reference and research about how they would look if they were real. Characterisation is my favourite thing to do when it comes to animating.

When people see my work and say "Yes, that's exactly how a creature with 7 tentacles, a head of a bat and wings of a dragon should look!!" – you know you've done your job and that's the best feeling.

If there was one thing you could say to past-you, what would it be?

I would say:

> Sankalp, relax and stop being stressed all the time about your work. Don't make work your life. I know this is your passion and that's why you came here. But that shouldn't stop you from going out and exploring a little or spending good time with your friends and family. You need to need understand the importance of switching off once in a while.

What's your top tip for someone starting out looking for a job?

I think one thing that people usually forget is that when your showreel is completed and you've applied to all the companies that you could, don't stop working on personal projects. Continuing to animate cool things while you're looking for a job will keep you motivated.

How did you find out about the job you're in now?

Google! I found the company who worked on "Switchblade" and my god, that game caught my eye. I've always loved MOBA (Multiplayer Online Battle Arena) games. I love playing "League of Legends" and when I saw Switchblade, which is a third-person MOBA game but with amazing vehicles, I was like this is the most unique thing and uniqueness always catches my eye. So, I applied, and I was lucky that they gave me a chance to prove myself.

What was the most important lesson you learned in your first year in the industry?

I had imposter syndrome during my first year. I always used to think that I don't belong here. I used to see other people working amazingly and I thought even if I try, I couldn't achieve that. It took time for me to realise that I'm here for a reason.

You've made it this far and you're surrounded by talented people. Don't hate yourself because your work doesn't look like theirs. Everyone is where they're supposed to be. Everyone has taken their first step onto the ladder and from there they've done great things. Now it's your turn.

What do you think is the most important quality of a game developer?

Keeping an open mind, ideas can come from anywhere.

I try to play or see gameplay of as many games as I can, regardless of their art style or which studio worked on it. Recently I played Tchia by Awaceb, I honestly didn't expect myself to love that game so much. It was one of the most beautiful games that I've played in a while; heart touching music, amazing mechanics and the best thing about the game was that I had the power to become anything. From creatures to non-living things – that's such a unique mechanic.

I think keeping an open mind always opens a door to new inspirations.

What would be your dream game to work on?

"God of War", I love everything about those games. Characters, creatures (my favourite) and the epic Boss fights. I love how smooth the games are and how they feel to play, especially the combat system. It has such a beautiful story of building a bond between a father and his son.

What would you need to do to make you feel like you've "made it"?

I think growing never stops. My goal right now is to create a character's full locomotion set, giving them a personality, setting them up inside the game and seeing people enjoy playing them. If I could make something that makes someone feel the way I felt when I played "Devil May Cry", that would make me feel like I've made it.

What does success look like to you?

My dream was to work in a game studio, making cool games with a team of people who wanted the same thing. It was my dream that came true.

I hope to one day lead a team; creative minds working together to make amazing games.

What do you do when you're having a bad day?

When having a bad day, I usually do a physical activity as they help me clear my head. I go swimming and instantly that puts me in a good mood. Then after coming back from swimming, I'll order food from my favourite restaurant to make me feel even better!

What is the best piece of advice you've received?

No matter how much you grow or how successful you are, don't forget your roots. Don't forget where you came from.

Final words?

Look for inspiration in everything. Keep yourself motivated and dedicated throughout the process, otherwise a simple animation will take super long. When you need to, give your brain a rest and come back to things with a fresh and new perspective, that will help you to see the mistakes better. When you can, animate what you want to animate because that way you'll have a drive to see what it will look like when it's finished!

Your First Day 7

7.1 FIRSTLY, YAY YOU!

You did it! You got the job! Sometimes you get so swept up in the progression that you fly through each step without fully processing them. It's important to take time to appreciate how hard you've worked and how far you've come. This is such a massive milestone in your life. Congratulations.

7.2 WHAT WILL BE EXPECTED OF YOU?

There are lots of misconceptions when it comes to what will be expected of you when you begin your first job as an animator. I'm going to answer some of the most common questions I've gotten.

Will I be expected to complete long, complicated sequences?

As a junior, you *should not* be given anything you can't handle. Good teams will ramp you up gradually and in line with your skill set. However, some teams may throw you in at the deep end. Juniors can sometimes be taken advantage of, it's important to recognise this and highlight if you aren't comfortable or are struggling.

Will I be expected to animate really quickly/Will I receive loads of deadlines immediately?

No. The important thing to learn as a junior is that quicker doesn't equal better. Understanding the fundamentals of animation is where juniors

DOI: 10.1201/9781003344841-7

should focus their efforts. You will get deadlines, how soon after your start date is dependent on the project demands but being a junior should be reflected in your time restraints.

Will I be expected to know how to use every piece of software?

No. Studios vary with what software they use and/or their way of working within that software. You should be shown or at least have access to documentation on how to use everything you need to do your job. If you don't know how to use a certain piece of software or how to do something, you will be given the time to learn. Always remember – don't suffer in silence – just ask.

Will I be expected to understand game engines?

Whilst it's preferable that candidates have some understanding of what a game engine is and the basics of how to navigate within one, it is not essential for a junior. If a core level of animation ability is demonstrated, we will teach our juniors everything they'll need to do their job, including but not limited to their interaction with the engine. Also, unless the studio works in Unreal Engine or Unity, it's impossible for you to know how their proprietary engine works.

7.3 UNDERSTANDING A GAME STUDIO

Something that hit me in the face when I started was how many different roles there are inside a game studio! I guess because I came from a VFX/Film course, there were so many departments I'd never heard of. I thought it might be a little useful to overview the main departments and *some* of the roles to expect, so you aren't as dumbfounded as I was!

7.3.1 Animation

The Vital Role of Technical Animators: *Gameplay animator, cinematic animator, technical animator, rigger*

Animators bring characters and creatures to life utilising their knowledge of fundamental animation principles to support gameplay and the overall feel of the game. Technical animators design, create and implement rigs, state machines, animation graphs, tools and workflows.

7.3.2 Art

The Role of Artists in Game Development: *Character artist, creature artist, concept artist, hard surface artist, vehicle artist, environment artist, lighting artist*

Artists are responsible for crafting the narrative experience through the creation of individual assets and the construction of entire worlds.

7.3.3 Technical Art and VFX

The Essential Role of Technical Artists: *Technical artist, technical character artist, VFX artist*

Technical artists are the glue between programmers and artists. Creating and implementing tools and workflows, managing game performance and creating artwork. VFX Artists create visual effects such as explosions, weather, lighting and magic using a combination of art and physics.

7.3.4 User Interface

The Role of Graphic Artists in Game User Interface (UI): *UI artist, UI designer, UX designer, motion designer, graphic artist, 2D art*

Responsible for creating on-screen graphics that help players digest critical information about the game through menus, buttons, icons, maps and feedback. They make sure that the game is clear, intuitive and consistent with the style and theme – without being intrusive.

7.3.5 Design

The Role of Vision Holders in Game Design Leadership: *Game designer, level designer, narrative designer, combat designer, technical designer, game director, creative director*

"Vision Holders" designers are responsible for steering and directing everyone's work towards making the most fun game whilst hitting the creative goals as defined by the creative director(s). They can take an idea, evaluate its failings and decide which elements are worth taking forward.

7.3.6 Programming

The Integral Role of Programmers in Game Development: *Programmer, animation programmer, gameplay programmer, physics programmer, network programmer, audio programmer, UI programmer, tools programmer, technical director*

Programmers write the code that builds the foundations to allow other departments to create – through engines, tools and gameplay systems. They also ensure the game is playable on various platforms whilst heading up optimisation efforts across the wider development team.

7.3.7 Production

The Multifaceted Role of Producers in Game Development: *Producer, assistant producer, associate producer, technical producer, production manager, development manager*

Supervise the development of a project from start to finish. Producers coordinate across departments, oversee the budget and schedule, ensure the quality and creativity of the final product meet with the expectations of the publisher and maintain the team's overall mental capacity/morale.

7.3.8 QA

The Role of Quality Assurance Testers in Game Development: *QA engineer, QA analyst, compliance tester, QA manager*

Work with developers to identify and test potential issues in the game design and implementation. They check how the game works from both a technical and a player perspective.

7.3.9 Analytics

The Role of Data Analysts in Game Development: *Data analyst, game analyst, user researcher*

Analyse data to gain insights into player behaviour, game performance and other key metrics. Alongside this, they present data in a digestible format to key stakeholders.

7.3.10 Community and Marketing

The Role of Community Managers in Game Engagement: *Community manager, social media manager, brand manager, marketing officer, copywriter, event manager, influencer marketing manager*

The bridge between the company and the players of the game. They communicate with both sides, create and share content and manage the online community spaces.

7.3.11 Operations and Human Resources

The Multifaceted Role of Human Resources Managers: *Maintenance and facilities, office manager, recruiter, human resources (HR) advisor, HR manager*

Manage and support the employees in aspects such as developing policies, providing advice and guidance, ensuring quality of office environment, organising events, maintaining employee records, hiring, orientation, training, motivating and retaining talent.

7.3.12 Finance

The Role of Studio Accountants in Game Development: *Finance assistant, finance manager*

Managing and reporting the financial performance and position of the studio. They carry out payroll, allocate the budget for game development, marketing, operations and other expenses.

7.4 GET TO KNOW YOUR TEAM!

Your team is the most integral part of your success. Of course, you can completely ignore them and try to go it alone but trust me, you won't last long. Either they've just begun too so you can help each other figure things out or they've been through it all before so every question you have, they already have the answer for. They've been in the industry for years and have more wisdom than you can fathom. They're assigning you work so get on their good side! That last one isn't *as* true, but it definitely helps to be honest with your lead/director with what you're comfortable with, what you enjoy, what you're struggling with – they don't know what you don't tell them.

Your team is your ally, the people you can go to when you have a problem, the people you can talk to if you're having a bad day, struggling with an idea or you just want a rant! The longer I'm in this industry, the more I realise that the most important thing to me is my team. They're the people you're going to see every day and work alongside, it really helps if you can have a laugh with them! What's better is if you can share with them, sometimes you're going to feel overwhelmed, frustrated, worthless, jealous, stupid, sad, it's nice to have a safe space to let that out in. You'd be surprised how often your teammates will be feeling the same!

Taking time to get to know the people on your team, their pet's name, their favourite film, when their birthday is, asking them about their family or what they did on the weekend. Some people will be more closed off than others and you'll quickly learn who they are, respect that. Remembering and referencing even the tiniest of details about people makes all the difference, being personable really does go a long way.

Interview With . . . Mike Waterworth | Principal Technical Animator/Wizard

Mike hired me! My first ever job interview consisted of me and Mike chatting for three hours about animation, rigs, stuff we like, stuff we hate – our conversations now are basically the same, maybe longer. The most generous man I've ever known, he is the type of person who will remember what kind of sweets you like and buy squeaky toys for your new puppy. Then on top of that, he's just the most talented yet humble guy – he was in the industry before the PlayStation! You name it, he's rigged it.

How did you get your first job in the industry?

I have been in the games industry for many, many years, kind of even before it was called an industry. It was a very different time back then to how it is now. I was lucky enough to get my first job from a great bloke called Jeff Bramfitt, a very skilled lead artist at Psygnosis. He saw my illustration work at my degree show in Liverpool, called me up and asked me if I wanted to come in and do an art test using Deluxe Paint on an Amiga. Hell yes. I had never really used a computer back then, but I struggled on and found I loved it, especially the sprite animation. The rest is history, literally history. All thanks to Jeff.

What was the most important lesson you learned in your first year in the industry?

Wow, my first year in the industry was a long time ago now, a lot of what I learned in that first year isn't so relevant anymore. It was almost a different world back then; no roles for designers or producers, almost constant crunch, whole games made in three months or so with just three or four people etc. However, I guess one of the most important lessons I learnt was that games should be fun and entertaining to play, and it is *all about the final game*. I also learned that making games isn't always fun even if it's a fun game. Development of a game can be a frustrating, struggle filled, with clashes and compromises. From a technical art and animation point of view, I quickly learnt the mantras of "whatever is required" and "for the good of the game". Even now though, I encounter artists who produce work like it is made for their showreel rather than made to fit within a game; assets that are overly complex for what is required. Technical Artists basically glue the art and code together to make the game possible, never forget that *it is all about the game* not about self-gratification or self-promotion.

I also learned pretty early on that it is important to take something positive from each project beyond the project itself as a whole. Always try to learn from any experience in a positive way.

If you were to go back to the beginning of your career, would you do anything differently?

I often joke that I think I should have become an animator or sculptor or something more artistic based. As their skills are more transferable between projects and aren't so linked with the ever-changing world of technology. Being a technical animator involves constant evaluation, learning and re-learning. This can make it a very tiring career if you don't enjoy the learning aspect of it and it can become very stressful if your employers don't give you time to learn and develop in work time.

My career and skill set evolved naturally alongside the demands of the industry, the availability of learning resources and the people I could learn from. Saying all this, would I have done anything differently? Probably not, as my path has mostly been steered by my personality – all I want is to keep things simple and help my teammates.

Have you made any mistakes that would have been avoidable "if you'd only known" that might help others to know?

I have probably made many mistakes over the years, but as game development is quite a slow and iterative process, the consequences of mistakes often get smoothed out over time. This is different for film or TV work, where the deadlines are more abrupt and thus less forgiving to mistakes. Although it's a bit corny to say, I believe failing is a massive part of learning. Technical animators deal with broken things all the time, it is our world, and we should be comfortable in it. Our daily process of evaluation means we are constantly looking for mistakes; mistakes we have made, or mistakes made by other people, then we mend them.

Saying all that, a common mistake I have encountered a lot throughout my career is legacy. This is when design for the game has evolved and advanced but the game systems to make that game haven't. This creates a mismatch where design and functionality clash and often a compromise is attempted, which usually doesn't work. Yep, legacy issues are bad but if the game is researched and developed correctly, this shouldn't be an issue. It is very important for technical animators to spot and flag legacy issues.

Who [or what] has been your biggest inspiration?

Over the years, I've learnt to recognise anything that inspires me and makes mental notes of them. It is an important skill to have to keep yourself motivated and sane. My inspirations come in many forms; comics, books,

games, art, films, TV, music, talented strangers on the internet, great people I've worked with or indeed are still working with, bad people I've
worked with or am still working with (yep, inspiration *not* to be like something is a powerful motivator too), and so on.

There are too many talented people I have worked with for me to mention here, but all of them I hold dear in my heart and am very thankful for
encountering them. They have helped make me, me.

What is the biggest mistake you see in job applications?

I've had bad interviews where a person has been arrogant or just plain rude
but luckily these aren't common.

One mistake I often see is people who apply for a position when they
don't know what they want to do. They come into the interview and say
they can do everything, which isn't bad, but they also say they *want* to do
everything, very different. The interview then turns into working out if
that applicant would be happy to do the specific role they've applied to do.

The worst mistake I have encountered, and it's not really a mistake, it's
just plain wrong. When an applicant shows work that isn't theirs and tries
to pass it off as their own. It's a real kick in the guts when you find out that
you have been duped by a liar in this way. There's an unspoken element of
trust that exists in the interview process, it's a big mistake to think you can
take advantage of this.

What do you think is the most important quality of a game developer?

Compromise, knowing when and how to reach a compromise will help
you to no end. Be friendly and approachable so your team wants to work
with you. Have respect for other people and respect for their role within
the process. Self-awareness, this doesn't have to be on a deep level, but just
recognising how you are feeling, both mentally and physically.

But most of all, you just need to *care* about the game you are making,
or at least, the part of it you are working on.

How technical do you feel animators should be?

In my experience, I consider gameplay animators to be quite technical.
Understanding the behaviour of the state machine in the game is intrinsic
with the creation of the animation cycles themselves. They need to be
technical enough to understand not only the software to make the animation but also how the animations are implemented within the game.

Day to day, I feel all animators should have a basic understanding of
technical aspects within the animation software they use. There are many
tools and features within animation software to aid the creation of the
animation. I'd expect an animator to know about constraints, IK and FK

systems within the character control rigs, keyframes, function curves, transferring and importing animation data etc. I would also expect them to understand what animation data the game requires and how to clean this data up for exporting into the game. They should also understand how to import animation data into the game engine they are using.

Do you have any recommendations for staying up to date with new technology and pipelines? [it can be quite overwhelming]

I follow quite a few people and companies online. I subscribe to what I find interesting and get notifications of anything newly posted. I try to make a bit of time in my busy day to scan over this stuff. I talk about anything cool I see with my peers and share my knowledge with others. Often people will return the sharing of knowledge by showing any cool stuff they have seen too. I watch organised talks from events such as GDC, SIGGRAPGH and AnimEx. Although these can take up quite a lot of time to catch up on, it is always great to see how someone facing the same issues as me has solved them.

I also watch reviews of newly launched games; these often talk about new tech they've used and give me a great jumping-off point to investigate!

How do you stay on top of your own personal progression?

I am lucky enough to work four days a week. Although this has been tough financially, it has given me the time needed to keep my current skills up to date whilst allowing me to learn and experiment with new ones.

I have used this day away from work to push myself into areas that have taken me out of my comfort zone; like teaching a workshop at a university or creating none-game specific rigging solutions for visualisation/rendering. Recently I worked with a very talented sculptor to design a workflow for collaborating on the construction of mechanical rigs whilst the asset is actively being designed and sculpted, instead of having to wait until the model has reached completion to begin the rigging process. This was called the Rig.B project and the final result was a humanoid robot character used by Autodesk which they then used to demonstrate its Live Link features between Maya and Unreal 5.

What would be your dream game to work on?

Easy. A turn-based multi-player strategy game of a firefighting robot trying to combat spreading fire like it's a living creature and rescue people and make that game world a safer place. All done in the design style of Jerry Anderson and inspired by the work of real-life firefighter Red Adair. This is a game I would just love to play and would really love to make.

What would you need to do to make you feel you've "made it"?

I will never feel like I've made it. That implies I've finished something and reached some sort of peak. I will always be looking upwards, ready for the next thing I need to understand.

Being recognised as a person who has "made it" isn't something I need for inspiration; I am blessed in that way. As long as the people in my team think I'm good, I'm happy.

What does success look like to you?

Success looks like a happy successful animation/rigging team who have a solid and robust pipeline and knowledge to use it to make great games.

Success is being respected enough to be approachable by anyone in the team, who will know I will help them and support them in any way I can. Success, I guess, means being good at my job.

What do you do when you're having a bad day?

I keep in mind that everyone has bad days, they are allowed. I raid my bank of inspiration material, often I just listen to some music (good to do) and have some snacks (bad to do). I will then go and rub my dog's belly and remind myself it's only a game, nothing life or death, and working on games is super cool. Then I work out a plan to get my bad day back to being a great day.

What is the best piece of advice you've received?

I was once told "Don't eat anything bigger than your head" that sounded like pretty good advice.

But regarding work, someone once told me not to bottle up feelings of stress or frustration. It sounds so obvious to just talk and express your concerns, but it can be hard to do. You have to be careful not to let issues fester over time and become negative. I evaluate the importance of issues I encounter and either confront them straight away or let them just melt away and move on.

My advice to others is that having a good chat is usually a positive and productive thing to do, so don't be afraid to do it.

Final words?

Strive to be happy.

Your First Month 8

So, you're over your first week; you know where the bathroom is, you managed to log into your work email and you're slowly figuring out what channels to join on slack. You've been introduced to what feels like a million people and you've forgotten everyone's name, that's fine – nobody remembers anyone's name in their first week. Maybe you're a little overwhelmed, that's natural, everything is very new and very daunting. Everyone else is so established and confident, it's not fully sunk in that you're *actually* an animator in a real-life game studio . . .

8.1 INTRODUCING . . . IMPOSTER SYNDROME

You know when you look around the office and think "How am I here?"

You're sitting next to someone with 20 years of experience, and you feel like you'll never compare. You don't deserve to be here.

You're given your first task and you have absolutely no idea where to begin.

You begin animating and you just feel embarrassed, you can't animate. You can't ask anyone for help because then they'll know how bad you are. You feel so completely out of your depth. It must have been a fluke that you got the job. They're going to figure it out any day now and come *fire you.*

Everyone you're comparing yourself to, that you think has it all figured out, almost definitely thought all the same things when they started too. Some of it never goes away. It's so common they gave it a name – Imposter Syndrome.

Defined as – *the persistent inability to believe that one's success is deserved or has been legitimately achieved as a result of one's own efforts or skills.*

DOI: 10.1201/9781003344841-8

But fear not, it does get better. The most daunting part of beginning your career is that it's all so new, you have nothing to compare it to, so of course you're going to doubt your ability to do it. The only thing you can do is give it time, as you get to grips with your new profession, you'll find that voice will quieten. The more you understand what you do, pushing yourself to learn new things and finding better ways of doing things, the more confidence you'll gain in yourself and the more you'll feel that you deserve to be exactly where you are.

8.2 #FRIDAYSOCIAL

Feeling isolated and disconnected from all the existing employees of the company is a super common occurrence. The best way of solving this is to get involved with some of the social groups your company will no doubt have. The variety and existence of these groups will depend on the size of the company and the number of employees who actually live locally. The classic is "Friday Drinks" after a long work week you will usually find people at the local pub. This is an ideal way to catch your colleagues with their guards down, outside of work mode and have an actual conversation with them. I'd also like to add that I know it's implied that you have to be into drinking to go but that isn't the case at all, it's completely socially acceptable to go along to Friday drinks and not drink. It's universally recognised as a space to get to know each other, have a rant, bond, gossip, debate. All those people you see around the office that seem so intimidating to speak to generally don't seem so scary outside of work!

Of course, the pub isn't for everyone, there *should* be more social groups than this alone. *Investigate your slack channels and ask around*, there will most likely be other groups you can participate in. These can range from sports to photography, usually people will try to find others at the company with similar interests that they can make into group outings. If you can't find the specific interest you're looking for, there's nothing to say you can't start your own group!

Other things you can do to help feel like part of your company's community is taking part in their events. Charity events, training days, workshops, local community events and parties. If your company asks for people to represent them or help out, *putting yourself forward* not only shows your willingness to the people who asked but also encourages others to put themselves forward. These events encourage your own self-development, you put yourself in a vulnerable position when you volunteer but you'll always be better off for it. Take on every experience you can, you have no idea what you'll get out of them.

8.3 FIND YOUR PEOPLE

The great thing about any of these social events is giving you the opportunity to feel part of something. To talk to people that you work directly with and people you don't. To find out about other projects at the company, why people do the roles they do, what brought them here, whether they enjoy what they're doing. Whilst also getting to know who tells the best stories, who knows all the gossip, who loves dogs and who hates pineapple on their pizza. The more people you can find common ground with, a little inside joke or a funny story will transform your perception of the office into such a warmer and friendlier place.

Once you do all this, you'll begin to find who your people are. These people may not necessarily be in your team but will help give you insight and perspective. The people you can go to if you have a technical problem, a random question or you need advice. You're going to have bad days and it's important to know who will get a hot chocolate with you and listen to your incessant moaning but it's also important to know who will be a voice of reason and help you come to rational conclusions.

Having an avenue to talk about things irrelevant to work is also completely viable. Something as simple as having a slack conversation that consists purely of cute cat videos and stupid memes is enough to ease stress throughout the day.

Having people within the company who have your back, that understand your problems and are having similar ones themselves, is really one of the best ways of keeping your sanity at work. I cannot recommend it enough.

Your First Year

9

Your first year is probably the hardest year you'll experience. There is so much for you to figure out and understand. You go into your first job in industry with a lot of expectations, dreams, fears, an idea of what you thought you wanted and where you thought you'd end up. That will change a lot in your first few years. The problem with all those ideas and opinions is that they were based on a very limited understanding of what the industry was going to be like. You really don't know what you'll enjoy working on, what kind of animator you'll want to be, whether you even like being an animator, until you get that experience first-hand. The main point I'm trying to make is don't have too many expectations of yourself going into this, approach everything with an open mind and trust the people around you. Gain all the insight you can from your team, the studio, the industry, listen to people, absorb everything and surrender yourself to the learning process.

9.1 BEING A JUNIOR IS *HARD!*

Life as a junior is super daunting. Everybody knows that. Luckily, everyone around you can relate to that because they've all been in your shoes. That ever-present feeling that the slightest mistake you make will get you fired. You are the least experienced and it's hard to fully acknowledge that. *To admit that you don't know.* But trust me, the sooner you embrace that the better off you'll be for it! You really are the only thing holding you back. The people who hired you are well aware of your skill set, they know you're a junior and that there will be a certain degree of getting you up to speed with how things work.

I think one of the biggest challenges of being any type of professional creative is how to navigate receiving critique. The thing with creative jobs is that you put your heart and soul into your work. The fact that we have the opportunity to do that is fantastic, please never be put off from doing that. That being said, the hardest thing is putting your all into something for it to not work, for someone to not like it or simply for it not fitting the brief. That's ok though. That's just part of the process. The great thing about animation is that you can get that answer pretty quickly. Something I wish I fully embraced sooner was to *get feedback early and often*. I used to gatekeep my work because I just never thought it was good enough to show. I was terrified that my director would see it and regret they hired me. I would work on simple animations for so much longer than I should have, only for it to have fundamental problems that would have been super easy and much simpler to fix in the first hour! The other important thing to note about critique is to not take it personally. The only way you'll improve is through actioning the feedback you receive, learning from it and actually understanding what was causing that issue in the first place. You'll find that the more you can anticipate what people are looking for in your critiques the smoother the whole process is. Just so you're aware, you will always need that critique stage no matter how senior of an animator you are, having a second pair of eyes sanity check your work will always be necessary! The main goal as a junior/mid travelling towards being a senior is to receive fewer notes on core mechanics and more on stylistic decisions.

9.2 BEING A JUNIOR IS *FUN!*

The funny thing about being a junior is how most of the pressure we feel is internally created. The most amazing part about being a junior is you have no responsibilities! I really wish that I let myself enjoy that more. There really is nothing to be scared of, you deserve to be exactly where you are, and you're allowed to have no idea what you're doing. Absorb everything, get involved in as much as you can, ask dumb questions (they probably aren't as dumb as you think), share your thoughts and opinions, take notes, record your screen when people show you how to do things (then you don't have ask them to show you again) and most importantly – enjoy it.

Interview With . . . Maximillian Shipley | Technical Animator

The first person to ever be officially "led" by me! Max is the best because I can hand him my cute animations, explain my grand visions of how I want them to fit together and then he'll make it all *actually work*.

What made you want to work in games?

I just liked playing games and found no other courses or subject choices that interested me. Eventually I ended up falling in love with working in engine and that's how I basically fell into technical animation . . .

What formal qualifications did you receive to become a technical animator? Do you think you need formal qualifications?

I studied Games Animation at Teesside University although I realised pretty early on in the course that animating wasn't for me. Personally, I don't think you need formal qualifications to make it as a technical animator, a very strong portfolio, an understanding of animation and experience with a game engine is what matters.

What do you like about being a technical animator?

Solving problems and making all the fancy animations that I couldn't make myself work in the game.

If there was one thing you could say to past-you, what would it be?

Learn Python scripting. As much as focusing on unreal has helped me I wish I had started learning scripting earlier as it opens up so many different avenues in tech animation.

What's your top tip for someone starting out looking for a job?

Just keep applying, I applied for Lucid twice! The job reappeared and in the months since the first application I had clearly improved my portfolio enough to get an interview.

How did you find out about the job you're in now?

I didn't know technical animation was a craft in itself until about a year before I got my job. All my projects at university were centred around engine work which led to one of my tutors suggesting that I look into technical animation as a job role. I then just looked around on different sites and social media for job postings until I landed one.

What was the most important lesson you learned in your first year in the industry?

Even the most talented industry veterans google things, no one magically knows everything and it's ok to not have all the answers.

What do you think is the most important quality of a game developer?

To be able to have fun and enjoy what they do.

What would be your dream game to work on?

I don't have a dream game but I always liked "Devil May Cry" so a hack and slash game would be cool at some point in my career.

What would you need to do to make you feel like you've "made it"?

Be a part of a game's early development and see it all the way through to its full release.

What does success look like to you?

I consider myself to have already succeeded just for the fact that I've moved away from where I grew up, doing a job that I love and working full time in the industry I always wanted to work in. Becoming a senior technical animator will be my next bit of success . . . P.S. Hollie, can I have a promotion?

What do you do when you're having a bad day?

I find meditation helps reset and ground me on a bad day. Setting aside some time to feel present helps clear my mind and usually gets the ideas flowing!

What is the best piece of advice you've received?

Don't be afraid to ask questions. I would often get bogged down trying to tackle issues alone, which is pointless when you have a team of very smart people around you – just ask.

Final words?

Sometimes there can be real challenges in this line of work, whether it's a particularly technical problem or something annoyingly frustrating that you know there will be a simple answer for. When times get tough, I like to have a good moan to whoever will listen, that usually calms me down. Taking regular breaks also helps. I'm a bit unconventional as I love Mondays, I come in with a clear head and it's usually my most productive day! My point being, don't be too hard on yourself, you'll solve it eventually.

Who Said Learning Is Bad?!

10

Seriously, who said that? Why are we so ashamed of not knowing things? That's surely the best way to approach anything. Admitting you don't know and striving to change that.

10.1 YOU DON'T KNOW WHAT YOU DON'T KNOW

It's a simple phrase. Nobody is born with all the knowledge in the world. Nobody walks into their first job knowing exactly what to do. What a waste of time it is to beat yourself up for not knowing something you've never learned! Approach everything with pure curiosity and enthusiasm.

10.2 EMBRACE MISTAKES

You're going to get things wrong. You're going to say the wrong thing. You're going to make silly decisions. You're not perfect. You just need to ensure you don't keep repeating the same mistakes. *Treat everything as a lesson learned*, don't dwell, just do better next time. Dealing with our errors, owning up to our flaws and taking responsibility for them not only develops our own personal growth but also contributes to a deeper, truer level of understanding.

DOI: 10.1201/9781003344841-10

10.3 BREAK IT DOWN

Tasks can definitely seem super overwhelming at times. This usually stems from looking too far ahead, thinking about the end result and how you can't possibly do it all. This is when the panic sets in and you have no idea where to begin!

. . . Here I am again, to tell you this is another thing that happens to us all.

The best thing you can do in this circumstance is break it down. Focusing on the outcome, how far away it is, and all the steps in between isn't conducive to a great day at work. *Concentrate on the first step*, only think about that one step until you're finished then move onto your next step and so on. *Directing your focus* on the immediate and not the overall end result. It sounds simple but it's often the simplest solutions that get ignored or forgotten about when you're stuck in the brain fog!

Interview With . . . Amanda Renfroe | Head of Animation

I've learned a lot from Amanda, not only in the subtle art of animation but also in topics like self-confidence and trusting your instincts, which can be super tough to talk about. It really helped me a lot in my very early years to have a rockstar like Amanda listen, understand and share her experiences of things I honestly thought were only in my head.

What formal qualifications did you receive to become an animator? Do you think you need formal qualifications?

I did take the path of a traditional college education. I attended SCAD (Savannah College of Art and Design) for four years and received a Bachelor of Fine Arts degree.

Regarding my opinion about formal qualifications, I would ask the individual who is considering becoming an animator, what type of environment do you learn best in? Going to a university for a degree, online schooling courses or being self-taught have their pros and cons in terms of their learning environments and logistics (location, degree, instructors etc.), but they all revolve around the same goal to become an animator.

These years are the most important years of our career. Getting the most out of any of these scenarios will be dependent on our drive to better ourselves creatively and professionally. Just because we decide to take one of these tracks doesn't mean that we automatically become great professional animators when we enter the industry. I heard Ted Ty say in a work presentation that there are thousands of bad drawings inside of us, so the quicker you get them out, the quicker you get to the good stuff. There are many bad animations we must get through to start creating good ones. When I was in college, I was animating personal shots outside of my school assignments. I would pick an area of animation I wanted to strengthen, pick a few-second dialogue that was between three and five seconds, shoot my reference and go. Then I would spend a few hours a day or on the weekends working on it and have my friends critique it. When I graduated from school, a good chunk of my animation pieces were personal ones. Even after graduating I continued to work on personal animations and improved my reel with each one. Doing these elevated my reel and stuck out to Jalil Sadool and Keith Lackey a year after graduating as an animator who had potential. Then the rest is history.

When you decide which environment you want to take, understand that what you get out of it comes from what you make of it.

What qualities do you look for when hiring a junior animator?

This should be read with the acknowledgment that this is my perspective of what I look for in a young animator based on my experience at Steamroller Animation and working with my mentor Jalil.

There are two parts that we look for when hiring: a solid understanding of body mechanics and poses, and someone honest and driven.

To offer some insight into the latter, when I first became a part of the interview process, I would see Jalil focus on asking questions about themselves rather than focusing on their animation. Time and time again I would see the interviewee be taken back as they came into the interview prepared to talk about their work rather than about themselves. For us, the animation is a small part of the conversation. Understanding who a person is and how they will fit into the team is of more importance. With each interview, I understood more and more the value of knowing who we were hiring. I stay true to this value today and find myself diving into questions that give me insight into their self-awareness, growth through failure and collaboration.

If you were to go back to the beginning of your career, would you do anything differently?

Nothing. I wouldn't change a thing. The triumphs, the failures and the people I connected with made me the person I am proud of today.

What is the biggest mistake you see in job applications?

The first 20 seconds of your demo reel is the most important part of any application in my opinion. The demo reel is what is going to bring attention to the rest of your application. You're only as strong as your weakest animation. This statement rings more and more true especially now that I have experienced being the one reviewing hundreds of demo reels.

Here are a few highlights that I feel are important for a well-structured demo reel:

Use Vimeo to host your demo reel. Less clicks to the reel the better.

Clean title cards – a solid colour, name and email are all you need.

Quality over quantity – better to have two quality pieces than five subpar and dated pieces.

Have a full body shot on your reel – this will showcase your understanding of body mechanics.

Overlay labels or logos on the bottom corners – this will offer the reviewer insight into whether an animation was mocap or keyframe or part of a production.

Do you have any recommendations for staying up to date with new technology and pipelines? [it can be quite overwhelming]

In university and the early years of my career, I ate, drank and slept animation-related content. It took me years to build my feed on Vimeo, X (formerly known as Twitter) and YouTube to give me the latest animation releases, lectures and demo reels. I was able to stay up to date with animation-relevant information that I would then study frame-by-frame and revisit often in an attempt to absorb into my eyes.

How do you stay on top of your own personal progression?

I check in with myself often. I take a look at how I'm doing as a leader in terms of problem-solving, communication and interaction. I recall examples of situations from the past two weeks that I felt I dealt well with and take note of the ones that I felt could have gone better. Creativity I'll challenge myself with creating training for the department. Something I can sink my mind into and geek out about. Other times it's grabbing a shot from somewhere (very sparingly nowadays). Something small to dust off the Maya muscle memory.

What does success look like to you?

Success for me is working with an amazing team that motivates me to become a better leader and creative every day.

What do you do when you're having a bad day?

A bad day is only a bad day. It's nothing more. One bad day does not represent me or my performance. Again . . . one bad day does NOT represent me or my performance.

I had to be consistently reminded of this by my mentor and close co-workers till I believed it. Once I started to believe it, I spent less time overthinking and self-criticising, and I was able to find a flow to reflect more effectively and efficiently . . . and in all honestly was happier to know that I would become someone better tomorrow. If I found myself cycling back into overthinking the situation, then I would remind myself of the future course of action I concluded to after self-reflecting earlier. If I was satisfied with it, then I knew what needed to be done so I'd quiet my thoughts and move along. That constant reminder allowed me to manage my emotions better and become a more confident leader and problem solver.

Final words?

Find others who will offer honest feedback about your work. It can be tough to hear at times, but consistently remind yourself that it's to make you a better animator.

This Is Not an Animation Textbook (. . . Let Me Just Give You a Few Tips Though)

11

There are plenty of opportunities for you to brush up on the theory behind animation, the 12 principles of animation and more in-depth texts specific to game implementation. There have been several specialist books published which have become staples to animator's bookshelves worldwide.

That being said, I'd like to take some time to mention a few things that became apparent to me early on in my career that I wish had sunk in *even earlier*!

11.1 FIND A WORKFLOW THAT SUITS YOU

The existence of different workflows was a massive game-changer for me. The ones I'd read about were "Straight Ahead" and "Pose to Pose" which are more classic approaches to your general style, not the physical method that you

DOI: 10.1201/9781003344841-11

can adopt in the 3D sense. Again, I'm super briefly going to summarise these things, I really recommend you research further into all of this to figure out what works for you.

- *Straight ahead* – this essentially means starting at the first pose on the first frame and animating each frame after the next.
- *Pose to pose* – whilst this means focusing on key poses throughout the sequence, solidifying those, then moving on to their in-betweens, then their in-betweens and so on.

In terms of computer animation, come the more applied approaches.

- *Copied pairs* – taking a pose, copying and keyframing that same pose for as long as you'd like your hold or certain limbs to hold whilst making other adjustments. This solidifies your limbs and negates the weird floaty-ness that comes when you don't key everything you want to stay put.[1]
- *Stepped blocking* – this simply is blocking your animation in stepped tangent curves, which only shows you the frames you have posed. This gives you a clean and simple preview of your posing.
- *Spline blocking* – blocking your animation in spline tangent curves, which lets you see the automated path your limbs will take in-between keyframes. This can be distracting at first but avoids the "big switch" from stepped into the spline.
- *Separating limbs* – getting the movement right in the hips/cog, with all other parts of the body either hidden or frozen, I've seen people do this with a cube too then copying it over. Getting that initial rhythm, timing and spacing locked in. This can be a super handy method for a larger or particularly action-packed scene. Once happy with their hips they'll move along the spine, on to the head. Optionally adding rough arm, leg, face poses along the way until they go completely on to their arm and leg pass. Finishing with overall polish and facial focus where applicable.

These are the main workflows I've seen but there will no doubt be plenty more. I am truly fascinated by all the different ways people work and find work for them.

The biggest piece of advice I have regardless of which workflow you adopt is to spend the majority of your time in blocking. Really finesse your posing and timing, add as many in-betweens as you want/can! The more effort and attention you put into that phase the more you'll reap the rewards in your spline and polish stages. Ultimately, **you** should be in control of your animation, not the software.

11.2 GOOD REFERENCE = GOOD ANIMATION[2]

Reference is really integral to getting realistic grounding in your animations, for such a long time I tried to animate straight out of my head, and it really is a waste of time. The idea that great animators *don't need* reference is another thing we get into our heads early on for no real reason, great animators use reference! It's an art form in itself to record *good* reference, it can be really daunting to get up in front of a camera and act something out but let's see if we can talk about a few things to make it easier.

- *It doesn't have to be you* – it doesn't make you any less of an animator if you ask to record someone else for your reference. Getting people who most resemble your character is ideal as their weight shifts and general mannerisms will be different from your own and can often give you little niceties you may not have thought of acting out.
- *Find a safe space* – you don't have to record yourself in the middle of the office, find a space you feel comfortable to let go and have some fun in! Recording reference should be seen as a fun alternative work task not a dreaded chore.
- *Put on some music* – the influence music can have over the way you move and getting you into a character's headspace is remarkable. We use music all the time on our motion capture shoots to get the actor's out of their heads, it works the same for reference!
- *Get in character* – I'm going to talk a little more about this later on but trying to get inside your character's head, in the context of the situation you need reference for will get you way more natural results than the pure mechanics of the movement. Think about how they would feel in that moment, how they would react to this scenario and what would be going through their head.
- *Don't think of specific poses to hit* – this follows on from the last point, thinking of your reference as a real-life situation and playing it out naturally. If you're in your head about specific poses you want to hit it will come across very robotic and forced, which will impact your animation.
- *It doesn't have to be perfect* – remember that reference is just a guide and most useful in getting that core movement true to form. Maybe you didn't hit the poses exactly how you wanted but that's where you as an animator can choose to translate your reference

however you'd like. You can do whatever you want with it. You can chop up and cut your clips together, mess around with the timing and spacing. The power of reference is you can really plan out your sequence before doing anything in Maya.

11.3 POSING

Animation is *just a bunch of poses*. Well, that's not strictly true, yes, it's poses but those poses need to string together with other poses to make a readable performance. You'll have more extreme poses and more subtle ones which again, must seamlessly flow through each other. Those poses also need to be thoughtfully posed to look appealing, strong, readable, comfortable and all with correct weighting. Observing the world around you and studying *what makes a strong pose* will considerably level up your animations.

Here's a list of the things that are constantly running through my mind when I'm posing my characters:

- *A-symmetry* – "twinning" where your arms are doing exactly the same thing or facial expressions that are completely symmetrical are not very appealing. Unless your character specifically needs to move symmetrically, try to ensure there's a contrast from one side of your character to the other.
- *Flow* – avoid isolated movement, remember that everything is connected. When anything in the body moves there will be reactions and counterbalances to that action, regardless of how small that may be. Make sure that every movement dissipates throughout the body, the hips and spine are big hitters for this, you want them to flow through each other.
- *Broken joints* – ankles and wrists. Keep an eye on uncomfortable leg and arm poses, your knee should always be aligned with your toe, your wrist should flow from your forearm.
- *Head* – you'll find that heads don't move much. They're often the focal point of your animations, where your eye gets drawn to the most. Where the head is jagged and all over the place, your animation will suffer. Solidifying your head, which usually stems from your hips and spine, will do wonders for your sequence.
- *Weight* – always check where the weight is. There will either be a more dominant foot that your hips will be over, or it will be balanced

somewhere in the middle, weight transfers are a little trickier but keeping track of your weight is essential.

- *Lines of action* – you should always strive to make your poses as dynamic and readable as possible. One way to test this is to see if you can draw a clear line of action through your character.
- *Silhouette* – keeping your silhouette in mind, a messy unclear silhouette will affect the readability of your animation. Try to present your limbs independently from the torso of the body where possible for the action.

11.4 ARCS

A general rule of thumb is that all your limbs will be moving in smooth arcs. Paying close attention to the hands, feet, head and hips you can quickly see when things are out of place when they suddenly jolt out of their arc.

One handy way of visualising your arcs is through enabling *motion trails*. Motion trails help you track a specific limb's movement through space by marking its location at each frame and then connecting these points up to show a path. If there's something catching your eye that you can't quite pinpoint, it will no doubt be found in these trails. Of course, motion trails are just an off-shoot of the curves in your graph editor, keeping track of both of these things within your animations will benefit you massively.

11.5 OVERLAP

It's important to not get too fixated on adding overlap to your limbs before you've solidified their core movement, this is something you should concentrate on more in your polish stages. Remember that everything is connected, getting caught up trying to add isolated rotations in your wrists and feet will only waste your time if it's not rooted in the base movement of the rest of the limb.

Provided you are happy with your base motion, adding overlap is a really enjoyable part of polish! This is when you can really exaggerate your arcs, creating lots of nice drag and follow-through all the way through to your fingers and toes!

However, overlap not only applies to the sweeping motions of arms and legs but is also paramount in enabling us to accentuate everything we do no matter how subtle or extreme. It's the reaction to energy entering and leaving the body. Unnatural movements stem from abruptly beginning and ending without any warning and anywhere for the energy to go. To avoid this, we add anticipations and settles.

Consider how the clavicles soak up a lot of energy on impact and where that energy goes. Clavicles are often left as an oversight when people begin animating but can help exaggerate and sell a lot of core movement. They're great for adding subtleties to even the tiniest of animations, like breathing!

NOTES

1 The Copied Pairs method can be adopted in both stepped and spline workflows. The biggest tip when posing in any format is to keep an eye on your graph editor. The big hiccups that can happen when switching tangents, and just generally in your spline posing, come from those curves in the graph editor arguing with each other! We always strive for smooth-as-caramel curves.
2 That's not strictly true but it'll certainly get you closer to a good animation than a bad reference will!

Get It in the Game

12

As a gameplay animator, it is paramount that you get your animation into the engine to test as soon as possible. Even in its most early and roughest stages, you can get an idea of whether something will work. This is the most efficient way to work, as not only does it prevent animation from being a blocker (ensuring other departments can begin their work with rough timing and concept) but it also prevents you from wasting time on an animation that fundamentally doesn't conform to the design.

12.1 IMPLEMENTATION

Getting your animation in the game early not only aids the larger flow of development but is also an integral part of your own workflow. Testing in the engine early on can help you lock down specific posing, timing and spacing, a lot of it is down to feel which you can only really understand when it's in the game.

Outside of testing the mechanic in isolation for general feel and readability of that specific animation, it's important to also test your mechanic in the context of how it is intended to work in the game. This means not only in the context of the environment but also in the flow of potentially several other animations. Gameplay animations need to knit together seamlessly, in multiple sequences and scenarios whilst reinforcing the intent of design.

12.2 TROUBLESHOOTING

Problem-solving is a key part of being a gameplay animator, animating is the first step but getting your animation to *work* in the engine isn't always as

DOI: 10.1201/9781003344841-12

simple. There are many things to look out for and consider when your animation isn't playing as intended (or isn't playing at all!).

- *Root marker* – problems often stem from the root marker, keep in mind that the root marker controls the capsule of your whole character in the engine, so it holds a lot of influence. Ensure you keep this as clean and consistent as possible, with data only in the necessary axes.
- *Tags/sync markers* – the existence of these, how they work and how much influence they have over your animations depend solely on how the system has been set up. This will differ between projects and studios but is another common root of where your problems may arise, if you've not added these tags or if you've put them in the wrong place. The best thing to do is find any documentation for the systems you're working with or talk to the person who set it up.
- *Communication* – when in doubt, ask. Don't try and guess how to do things or try to force something together manually. Doing this runs the risk of breaking other people's work and the build-all-together. Systems are put together intentionally, find out how they work and what you need to do to get the results you want.
- *Dirty data* – sometimes you simply need to re-export your animation. The hardware/software/script you're using may have a hiccup from time to time, for no real reason. If your exports continue not exporting as expected, then you must bring this to the attention of the person who made the rig as this could be a sign of a deeper issue.
- *Checkbox* – this is a bit of an industry joke as sometimes you can spend a long time trying to get to the bottom of a problem. You've gone over your whole process; re-done the whole thing and you can't see any reason why it doesn't look right. Only for it to be a tiny checkbox somewhere you completely overlooked! Sometimes the answer is as annoyingly simple as that.
- *Don't suffer in silence* – if you experience issues technical or otherwise, it's important for you to bring this up with someone who can help you fix it or help you find the person who can fix it. Often, we try to solve things ourselves which is a great quality to have but fundamental bugs in tools/rigs need to be brought up to save the rest of your team from experiencing the same issues (and inadvertently each person coming up with their own workarounds!). These processes are developed intentionally to

speed up our workflows, it's part of the process for user testing to result in further development.

• *Make notes* – make a note of any solutions you find that work or update relevant documentation. Often the same problems re-surface, whether that be for you or for other people, so a solution you've found will save someone else looking for it in the future.

In the words of my dad: "Don't struggle if you don't have to!"

Interview With . . . Matt Lake | Lead Technical Animator

I've heard technical animators be referred to as Unicorns, that being the case, Matt is the most magical unicorn you could wish for! We both started in the industry at a similar time, we worked together on Destruction All-Stars, both gave talks at AnimX and are now both writing books. . . . Where our paths may differ, our trajectories have been weirdly aligned and it's been cool having someone to panic with about it all!

What made you want to work in games?

I grew up with Disney – my Nana had tons of VHS tapes for all the original Disney animated movies I watched "Bambi", "Robin Hood" and "Jungle Book". religiously as a child (and now). The penny was in the air for animation as a career until I was in my tweens, when I began to discover the world of cinematic narrative video games.

Games like "Halo 2" and "Max Payne" blew me away, I'd never experienced narratives on that scale before. These experiences weren't just stories like in a movie, they were also interactive, the best of both mediums combined.

My love for this cinematic trend in games has only gotten richer over the years with stellar experiences like "Last of Us" and the "Death Stranding". I began making YouTube videos and started creating Machinimas (Machine Cinema = making movies in games) as I really loved telling stories, and, at the time, Machinimas were the only medium I had access to tell these stories. As I grew older, more tools became more accessible to me, then this naturally transitioned back into the roots of the inspiration. I love characters, I love their struggles and strife, the challenges they face and what they have to do to overcome them. I love stories, and I really wanted to be a storyteller. I would love to one day inspire someone the same way Bungie and Remedy's masterpieces inspired me and still inspire me to this day. That's why I got into games.

What formal qualifications did you receive to become a technical animator? Do you need formal qualifications to get a technical animator role?

I studied a two-year BTEC college course in Computer Games Development, then studied Game Animation at Teesside University.

I don't think there's a yes or no answer, no matter what people will tell you it's certainly not a cut-and-dry answer. A qualification, whether that's a diploma, bachelor's, master's or even a PhD, is not going to hand you a job on a platter – this simply does not happen.

Would I be working as a technical animator without my qualifications? Definitely not. Do you *need* formal qualifications to get a job? Also, definitely not.

It does appear to be the most common method for developers getting into the industry these days though, in my experience most developers I know in their 20s and early 30s got into the games industry after graduating from university, but there are exceptions that didn't go to university or even college. While there are many who did get into the industry after graduating, there is a degree of survivorship bias, there are likely just as many people who never broke into the industry after graduating.

I think the important distinction for people to note is that with qualifications, the scrap of paper with your name on it is not going to get you a job – you get you the job. Your personality, your abilities and your portfolio get you the job. In many cases, you only get many of these things from completing courses and university degrees, as they give you the time and opportunities to develop your skills and grow as an individual; it's the most game-dev-like environment you can get without being an actual dev.

Something to keep in mind if you plan to work abroad is that you need formal qualifications to get a Visa.

If I was asked whether I recommend university; I definitely say I do. I loved my time there, it gave me access to some amazing facilities and equipment, the courses gave me project-based tasks that helped me improve areas outside of my comfort zone. It wasn't a personal project that I could avoid – this caused a lot of growth in me. I also got to work first-hand with a lot of students and lecturers to experience project-based workflows. This provided me with the experience to see the positives and learn how to navigate the negatives. I wouldn't have had the time to grow my skills and self if I hadn't done the courses I did, and I'm glad I did. Although I'm not over the moon about my tuition fees, however, both can be true simultaneously.

What do you like about being a technical animator?

My favourite part of the role is the variety; technical animation touches so many areas and works between many departments holding them together – one day you may be doing skeletal rigging and creating a dynamic skirt, the next day you may be creating some tools for the team to automate and improve workflow, then the next you could be in the engine making a state machine. Truly I find this variety the best part of the job, it keeps the work fresh and you don't get stuck doing the same task day in and day out.

If there was one thing you could say to past-you, what would it be?

I'd say to keep at it – the long nights and hard work pays off in the long run. I'd like to think my younger self would be proud of where I am now and wouldn't want to change the direction of that ship.

What's your top tip for someone starting out looking for a job?

Get yourself out there and in front of people. Whether that's sharing your work online or at networking events – the latter is where I struck gold and got my first job opportunity in games.

How did you find out about the job you're in now?

For my current employment, I was made aware of the opportunity by a friend I had worked with at another studio; they needed a technical animator and let me know about the role and the project. I loved working with them previously, and the work involved with the role was exciting with new challenges, so I jumped at the chance.

What was the most important lesson you learned in your first year in the industry?

The biggest lesson I learnt was that no one expects you to always know everything. You don't always have to have all the answers, that's what teams are for. The game industry is such a welcoming, warming and nurturing place – everyone is very supportive, and you don't need to hold the weight of the universe on your shoulders. Sometimes it's okay to not know something.

What do you think is the most important quality of a game developer?

The biggest trait that unilaterally applies to all developers is adaptability, if you can't adapt easily, you'll have a hard time. The industry is forever evolving, so you always have to be learning. If a problem arises, you can't chuck your hands up and forget about it, you must adapt to the situation and work with what you have to get the end result. Game development is a treadmill of ever-evolving technology, which comes with new problems and new processes.

What would be your dream game to work on?

What I would consider my dream game would be more of a dream project *and* team. I think the people you get to work and collaborate with are a big factor in what defines a dream game. Building cool stuff with cool people is the dream.

However, if I *had* to pick a project, it would likely be a cosy farm simulator – basically Viva Pinata.

What would you need to do to make you feel like you've "made it"?

The day you are comfortable is when I'd consider you've made it. Being able to wake up in the morning and not hate going to work or hate the people you work with; I'd say that is a very privileged and lucky position to be in. There are very few people in the world who can say they like going to work, so don't take that for granted if you work in the games industry!
Not only in work but being able to enjoy your own life too – having a nice work balance, having a comfortable income that you don't struggle month to month, and you get to work to live, not live to work. That's the dream.

What does success look like to you?

Contentedness is what I'd call a success state. That above all else – no money, fame, title, project or pedigree can bring contentedness.

What do you do when you're having a bad day?

The first step to having a bad day is recognising you're having a bad day. Once you've acknowledged that, you must accept that sometimes you can't fix it. People aren't designed to be always hitting 100% capacity, and that is ok. Productivity comes in waves, sometimes you'll do 100%, sometimes you'll do 10% – the important part is that you're consistent. Sometimes things just don't work out on a bad day, you hit problem after problem, or your brain just doesn't work and on those occasions, you may need to take a step back to clear your head to get a fresh perspective.

One thing to keep in mind is that small incremental effort over time makes a huge difference. Game development, while not physically intensive (unless you're doing mocap), is mentally exhausting – make sure to recharge those batteries.

What is the best piece of advice you've received?

"Dude, sucking at something is the first step towards being sorta good at something" – "Jake the Dog", "Adventure Time".

This quote is wise on so many levels. No one is born an amazing artist. No one is born an insane animator. No one is born fluent in C++. Just give it a try; you may suck at it. You'll probably suck really bad at it. But keep going – because one day, you might not suck.

Final words?

Good luck on this great adventure and, most importantly, have fun! <3

What Do I Animate?

13

The real struggle of being an animator is coming up with what you want to animate. It sounds simple but it can be really hard to generate ideas and find inspiration, especially if you're struggling to resonate with the character. Sometimes what can be really tough is if there's no real character, whether it's a mannequin or a generic object, these can be hard to invest in but as an animator, you can give anything life and purpose even if it never leaves your head.

13.1 UNDERSTAND YOUR CHARACTER

Get to know your character the same way you would a friend. Where are they from? Do they get on with their parents? How old are they? What are their hobbies and interests? Are they a cat or a dog person? Are they introverted or extroverted?

Through understanding who your character is you can begin to see the world through their eyes. This can help with narrowing down what kind of movements they would do, how they would stand and how they would approach life.

13.2 WHAT IS THE PURPOSE?

Put yourself in your character's headspace and in the scenario you're looking to animate. How would they react to this situation? Would they be happy, sad, indifferent, shut off or angry? Would they make direct eye contact? Would they

DOI: 10.1201/9781003344841-13

move their body with purpose or regrettably slump their way over? Would they enjoy attention being on them or try to make themselves as small as possible?

Giving yourself a persona and a context, you can begin to come up with more natural and lifelike ideas that you maybe wouldn't have thought of before (and it's hopefully a little less daunting!). When you're trying to force ideas and not really think about the character or the situational factors, you often come up with mundane and generic or massively caricatured movements that can come across unnatural.

13.3 GET INSPIRED

There are so many different avenues you can explore this process with to further support building your character's personality and aid your idea creation.

- *Research* – gathering existing reference is the natural first step as you begin to figure out who your character is. The wondrous thing about the internet is that it really does have everything, you just need to know what to search for. The problem with this is that you're limited to whatever your brain can think of. This is where we can use the internet's intrusive algorithms to our advantage – as soon as you watch a video on YouTube it will recommend similar videos therefore the more you watch, the more potentially useful references will come up. The great thing about this is that it will suggest things you have never heard of, you're essentially creating an account for your character and seeing what their homepage would say about them!
- *Music* – figure out what music your character would listen to, create a playlist specifically for that character. Music is so powerful in how it can affect your mood, playing music your character likes whilst recording reference really helps you loosen up and get into a certain headspace!
- *Mood boards* – collating picture references of certain styles, aesthetics, TV/film influences and popular figures that may resemble this character both superficially and for desirable mannerisms. Further to this, moving mood boards are a great way of visually representing a plan for how you'd like a character to look and feel. A page filled with small looping clips of specific references for core animations you're planning on; idle, walk, run, attack, jump, relevant transitions, emotes and general "personality moments" that you'd like to build in or just give general inspiration.

- *Personality types* – using the Myers-Briggs Type Indicator and inspired resources online, you can narrow down and differentiate between characters by figuring out what personality type they are. From this, you can construct a more detailed analysis of your character with several jumping off points for your research such as their strengths, weaknesses, potential career paths and popular figures that share the same personality type.

Interview With . . . Kristjan Zadziuk | Animation Director

I credit where I am in my career to Kristjan. He's been the most incredible mentor I could have ever imagined, never without a life lesson in the form of a random metaphor or an anecdote about his son Kamran. He has always pushed me to be my best, supported me, ranted with me, fought for me and if your boss doesn't do all those things – find a new one!

What made you want to become an animator?

I used to mess around with my parents' camcorder when I was younger (probably about 9–10 years old) experimenting with stop motion, animating my sisters' soft toys fighting each other just for fun. Then when I managed to get an Amiga 500 I would animate pixels jumping off buildings and through scenes in Deluxe Paint 3 for hours on end. I never saved any of them unfortunately, so I would just animate the same thing repeatedly. I think I've always "known" but hadn't realised that it was a possible career path until I started my A-Levels.

How did you get your first job in the industry?

Picture this: a small studio in Bristol, where dreams were big, and my ambitions were even bigger.

Now, rewind a bit. I had a brief stint at Aardman Animation post-university animating foliage and background assets, but stop motion wasn't doing it for me, and the film industry seemed more unpredictable than a weather forecast.

There was a persistent recruiter bombarding me with calls like there was no tomorrow. Apparently, my knack for modelling, animating and rigging had this studio in Bristol interested in hiring me. Eventually, I caved and said yes to an interview. Stepping into the studio, I found myself face-to-face with industry veterans. They had a mission for me . . . become a generalist on "Who Wants to Be a Millionaire". My main task? Bring the TV show's sets to life in 3ds Max, wasn't exactly a dream job, but the money was good, and thanks to the sales over Christmas, I snagged a hefty bonus after just six months. I thought I hit the jackpot, only to realise later that Christmas magic doesn't happen all year round.

The work was a breeze, but not exactly my dream gig. After all, I wanted to be an animator, but there was this producer at the studio who thought he was an animator too. He thought animation was easy and that they didn't need to hire an animator. He basically told me, "Nope, we don't need you to animate". Fast forward a bit, and surprise, surprise – that same producer got the boot for being a toxic tornado to the team. Call it karma or a twist of fate, but suddenly I found myself promoted to animator on the studio's next project. . . . In about a year, I went from zero to hero, becoming the go-to animator.

Thing is, I was navigating uncharted waters. No one taught me how to build animation systems, and I was basically making it up as I went along, the company also made RTS games and wasn't used to player-controlled characters. It was a wild ride, the industry has transformed since then, but those early days? They were like a rollercoaster with no safety instructions.

What qualities do you look for when hiring a junior animator?

Showreel first and foremost. If the quality of work isn't at the necessary standard, there is no real reason to move to the next stage, it's the first thing we see so make it count.

When it comes to the interview, I look for enthusiasm, communication and team fit. It is safe to assume that if we are interviewing you, we think you are skilled enough to do the job we are asking of you. The next thing we need to know is if you will be able to communicate, collaborate and connect with your peers, seniors and other game developers. *Especially* in the new climate of hybrid working. I think communication skills are more important now than ever, so we need to see that you can be comfortable with us and us with you.

If there was one thing you could say to past-you, what would it be?

Learn when to say no. I remember I used to say yes to everything, regardless of what it would mean, I would also underestimate the amount of work something would take to get a quality result. I would often deliver things quickly, but at low quality. As I got more experienced, I would take a little more time to check my work and focus on the craft. No one remembers how fast you work if your work isn't good, they only remember the pieces that were of high quality.

What's your top tip for someone starting out looking for a job?

Tailor your showreel to the job you want and the studio you are applying to. For example, if you want to work in games, show me game-oriented work. Show me what you can do with a loop, or how you put something together, if you want to work in film show performance and subtle actions. If a cinematic showreel comes to me and I'm looking for a senior gameplay animator there is a good chance it won't progress as that isn't the role we are looking to fill.

Also, if you are applying for a job directly, show a little respect to the studio. If possible, try and find out a little about what they have done or who works there, a little research goes a long way to making you stand out to us.

Is there something you particularly like to see in a person's showreel?

We can see if you can animate within the first 20 seconds of your reel, so focus on the craft of animation. I've seen hundreds of walk cycles and parkour scenes, so try to do something a little different with them. Try putting a twist on the regular walk cycle, an injured cycle for instance. If you are applying for games jobs, I love to see in-engine assets and how you would implement them. This shows an understanding of the process in context, alongside your animation ability.

What was the most important lesson you learned in your first year in the industry?

Absorb as much as you can, ask questions and get involved. You don't know what you don't know. No one expects much from you at the start so it's the perfect time to learn. The more experience you get and the more senior you become the less time you have for it. Don't be worried about showing your work to your peers and seniors, the good ones are there to offer feedback, support and encouragement. Not showing your work can make it seem like you don't care about what others think.

Have you made any mistakes that would have been avoidable "if you'd only known" that might help others to know?

The mistakes you encounter and how you learn from them is how you improve, so I see them as learning experiences. If you don't learn from those mistakes that is more of an issue in my opinion. But with regard to your question of "If you'd only known" I think I would have moved on from my first job earlier than I did. It wasn't clear to me then that the loyalty I gave them wasn't the same value they had for me. That studio took advantage of my goodwill and inexperience, ending up with me in the hospital. The way that studio reacted to my hospitalisation, for which I had been trying to hit a deadline, was what made me realise.

Who [or what] has been your biggest inspiration?

Professionally, that's an easy one, my first real animation director – Alex Drouin at Ubisoft was everything I wanted to be, creative, skilled, knowledgeable and respected. He showed me how to collaborate with others outside of animation and introduced me to how to look at gameplay systems the right way. He loved to iterate and tinker with systems, so they felt just right and had this uncanny ability to improve any of your animations with a few simple tweaks. It was one of the proudest moments of my early career when he approved one of my animations on my first try.

What is the biggest mistake you see in job applications?

Lack of focus on the quality of the animation work, too much focus on camera moves and rigs. The clue is in the title . . . animator. I'm also not a big fan of rating your skill level out of five or ten on a CV, as that is very subjective. I guess it just shows your confidence level with software, but the thing that catches our attention is the quality of your work.

What do you think is the most important quality of a game developer?

Communication, collaboration and connection, the new 3Cs. You must be able to show what you are thinking, how you are doing it and be willing to change and adapt to the needs of the project and those around you. With remote work, it's easy to become less visible and this can be seen as an unwillingness to get involved.

How technical do you feel you need to be as an animator?

Depends on where you are in your career, any technical understanding or at least a willingness to be open to the technical aspect of animation is useful when you are in the early stages of your career. At my level, I have an understanding of the technical aspects, but I don't need to worry about it as much as there are others much more talented around me to take care of that. I like to remove as many of the technical barriers as possible for my team, allowing them to focus on animation. The running joke at a previous studio I worked at was "Animators just wanna animate, yo" I stick by this, as too many technical barriers can slow down creativity.

Do you have any recommendations for staying up to date with new technology and pipelines? [it can be quite overwhelming]

You won't be able to do all of it to the level you want, so pick your battles and focus on the areas that interest you. Surround yourself with smart people that can help explain areas you're interested in learning more about. Social media has endless amounts of innovation and information, so that is a great place to stay up to date with the latest goings on. I also tend to have regular calls with my animation peers outside of my current studio, where we just catch up on all the latest goings on. This started during the pandemic when we couldn't all attend GDC for the animation boot camps.

How do you stay on top of your own personal progression?

Progression can mean different things to different people, I've been an animation director for over 12 years, but my progression is gauged differently now. I feel my communication skills and overall games industry knowledge have naturally grown over the years. I'm always open to new techniques and pipeline improvements and I'm always looking to find better ways to lead my team. Unfortunately, I don't animate as much as I used to, but I really enjoy passing knowledge to my team and seeing them progress. I want to build something that I'm proud of and be an inspiration to others.

What would be your dream game to work on?

I'm very lucky that I worked on it. ... The original "Assassin's Creed" if I hadn't worked on it, it would have been the game that inspired me to do what I do. I love games that break down barriers, push animation and take interaction to the next level. I also love the work of Playdead and Insomniac, they both have a heavy focus on fun and animation without compromising gameplay.

What would you need to do to make you feel you've "made it"?

I don't know if I ever will. The first time I spoke at GDC people were finding me afterwards to ask me questions about my job, seeing that they wanted to be in my position made me realise that I was very lucky to be where I was. However, I don't think you should chase that feeling of "I've made it", otherwise the next thing you know your entire career will have passed you by and you won't have enjoyed any of it.

What does success look like to you?

Enjoying my job and having a solid work/life balance is important to me, I never want to dread Mondays.

Enjoy your job, work hard, be passionate about learning and push to be better than you were yesterday. In doing this, you will find yourself in a better place and the traditional forms of success will follow.

What do you do when you're having a bad day?

Step away . . . go to the gym . . . go for a walk, but do not sit at your desk and wallow. The pandemic saw me have more of these than normal and it made me realise how much I missed human connection and interaction. I'm not the best at dealing with the pressure of having a bad day, but I'm learning how to deal with it better.

Final words?

Enjoy the ride, find what you love and become great at that because you are more talented than you realise.

Approaching Game Systems

14

Super quick reminder, as with the rest of this book, I will not be attempting to detail any specific methodologies in the development of game systems and their mechanics. There are comprehensive guides dedicated to breaking down and intricately explaining this very complex subject. My intention for this section is purely to offer up some tips and words of advice that have helped me and I hope can help you!

14.1 EMBRACE THE INEXPERIENCE

The great thing about having no experience *is* having no experience.

You have the ability to see things in a completely different light than the people who have been doing this for years. This perspective can be quite refreshing as your thoughts and opinions will differ from that of your team's because you're not bound to any one way of working or understanding of what will or won't work. In some respects, there is a degree of constraint that comes with gaining experience and knowledge as people will tend to opt for what is safe and familiar. As you gain experience, you will naturally be drawn to preferred methods and be able to offer a more constructive approach to your intentions.

However, before you reach that stage, your current outlook is just as critical. Of course, not all your ideas will be great or even possible but the important thing to keep in mind is that ideas can come from anywhere and anybody. A fresh outlook without the burden of foresight is something to be

DOI: 10.1201/9781003344841-14

taken advantage of, don't let anyone make you feel like your ideas aren't valid or worth listening to.

I have a fun story to back this up, the first time I worked on a character select screen. In my first year, my director asked me to put together some placeholder animations to support putting our first character into a selection menu. He told me to create an appear, idle, select, selected idle and de-select going back to the idle.

The appear was the first personality moment you'd see of a character so something short and sweet that transitions into the idle. The idle was a looping animation that showed subtle personality. The select would happen when you select that character, another personality moment that transitions to the selected idle which was a more active looping animation. Then a de-select, if the player decided to choose a different character, which would transition from selected idle back into the regular idle.

My director was expecting a simple transition for the de-select, going from one pose to the other. However, excited by my newly adopted process (that helped me considerably) with putting myself into the headspace of said character, I did just that. For each one of the animations, I thought "What would she do as a camera focused on her? How would she feel if she'd just been picked? How would she feel if she was de-selected?" I figured she'd feel sad if someone had chosen her and then chose to abandon her. . . . So, I animated her sad initially but then she brushes it off and goes into her regular idle.

When I showed my director my first pass of all these animations, he immediately asked if his eyes were deceiving him or if she was actually sad in the de-select, he loved it. We put these animations in the next playtest and (when we told people to de-select her) everyone on the team loved her reaction too! We went on to add a unique de-select for every character and it turned out to be a really cool opportunity to show more of the character's personalities. I loved that we had these special moments just waiting to be discovered all because I hadn't animated a character select menu before, didn't have much knowledge of menus in games as a whole and very briefly understood how to put a game system together.

14.2 WHAT WOULD LOOK COOL?

The way we devise our ideas can often be confining without us realising that we're doing it. How often do you dismiss your ideas internally without saying anything out loud because you think they won't be possible; they sound silly or assumed someone else must have already come up with the same thing? Limiting our imaginations before we've even entertained their feasibility sabotages the possibility of producing something truly sensational. That may sound dramatic, but this is the core of what makes game development so exhilarating!

The brainstorming process should be a completely open, safe and super exciting space to be in where you can suggest ideas, bounce off other people's ideas and create new ones from all the discussion! An idea doesn't have to be a fully thought out and assured *will work first time* in-engine concept. The beauty of gameplay is that you can try all sorts of stuff out, *nothing* is 100% foolproof but it's from those trials and tribulations that you get to come up with innovative, immersive ways of doing things!

With that in mind, think about what would make this moment truly mesmerising! This doesn't have to mean a big elaborate performance either, it's the completely ordinary fidgets and underrated expressions we overlook in life that can add so much realism to a game. Put yourself in the scenario of this situation happening in real life, as your character, what would *they* do? Fitting it into a system and how you break that down can all come later. The most fluid and natural mechanics come from unrestricted ideas that begin with "wouldn't it be cool if . . .".

14.3 BREAK IT DOWN #PART2

As we've previously mentioned, the least intimidating way to solve a problem is to break it down. This applies just the same to game systems.

A mechanic is an action; a system is a series of mechanics specific to a certain purpose. For example, throwing a punch is a mechanic which would belong to the combat system. Typically, mechanics have a beginning, middle and ending, these transitions must support the previous and proceeding animation. States dictate when a system gets triggered, if the character is relaxed, alert, moving, falling etc.

When creating a new mechanic or system, it helps to consider the following.

14.3.1 Context

When and where will this system get triggered? This provides environmental and situational factors you'll need to adhere to.

How often will a specific mechanic be seen? It's important to distinguish what mechanics the player will see the most as these will run the risk of feeling repetitive and will be the highest priority for polishing and adding variation.

14.3.2 Time

How long do you have to carry out specific mechanics, is there a frame restriction? Clarifying with design and considering existing similar mechanic frame ranges will help you to determine this. Not only will this reinforce readability and consistency of gameplay but it also avoids wasting time unnecessarily animating.

14.3.3 Interruptions

Can the player interrupt any part of the mechanic? It helps to distinguish what parts of a mechanic (if any) need to be interruptible as this affects what you can animate within a reasonable space so as not to look too unnatural in a quick transition.

14.3.4 Flow

What happens before and after? The aim of gameplay is to be as seamless as possible, it's integral that you understand what sequence a mechanic can possibly be played in. With this, you can establish what transitions a mechanic will require and what you'll be able to get away with.

Having a Bad Day?

15

15.1 EVERYBODY HAS BAD DAYS

Always remember this. No matter how long you've been in the industry, the directors, CEOs, your lead, the person sitting next to you, all of them have bad days just like you do. Sometimes things just don't work no matter how hard you try to make them, sometimes the simplest of tasks seem impossible, sometimes your head just isn't in it and that is completely fine.

It's how we respond to those bad days that's important. It may seem like the only option is to try and force yourself into a better headspace, glaring at your screen, trying to animate whilst inadvertently getting yourself more frustrated. It won't help you or your team if you sit brewing for the whole day because you have the potential to be unnecessarily destructive to your work, and anything you do produce you would no doubt be able to carry out at a much higher standard in much less time with a clearer mindset.

Depending on the degree of your bad mood, acknowledging it's there and attempting to clear your head is a much better use of your time. We're programmed to constantly keep up appearances of being productive and to feel guilty if we're not seen being productive but this whole mentality is counterintuitive. Taking time for yourself is the best thing you can do for your productivity, obviously within reason, you can't just give yourself the day off without telling anyone. Fortunately, mental health and the respective support it requires is becoming a crucial part of company policies across the world. Ask about your company's policies and what support they offer. For example, "mental health days" exist, no explanation is necessary sometimes you just need a day, and these are intended to support any person who is struggling.

DOI: 10.1201/9781003344841-15

15.2 WHAT TO DO WHEN . . . YOU FORGET HOW TO ANIMATE/ EVERYTHING IS BROKEN/YOU HATE EVERYTHING/NOTHING IS WORKING AND YOU SHOULD JUST QUIT NOW?!?!??!?!!

First things first, don't panic and stop spiralling. You're not a bad animator and one day of not-so-great animation isn't a meaningful reflection of your skill set.

- *Go outside* – get up and go for a walk, fresh air helps. A little distance from your desk and the same couple of pixels you've been fixating on for the last hour can do wonders for the soul.
- *Talk to someone* – rant to your teammates, see what other people are up to, talk about something unrelated, have a laugh about something completely ridiculous. It can be therapeutic to talk about how you're feeling or just talking generally, it'll take your mind off being annoyed.
- *Ask for feedback* – sometimes you can simply be too wrapped up in your own head, focusing on problems that aren't there or unintentionally making more problems for yourself. You can put off asking for feedback, especially if you're in a bad mood, but most of the time you'll feel better and clearer by asking sooner rather than later.
- *Refresh your memory* – refer back to your research and reference stages. Look through your mood boards, listen to their music, re-engage with who your character is.
- *Get inspired* – a lack of inspiration and motivation is often the problem. Step back from the whole thing, being so engrossed in your character and animating can be exhausting. Find what inspires you, not just for this specific animation or character but for animation and movement in general. I love watching dance and ballet choreography videos when my brain times out because it feels kind of productive but without the pressure of looking for a specific reference.

Interview With . . . Steve Bouliane | Animation Director

With Steve's more cinematic approach to animation, beginning his career in movies, I thought he'd be a really fabulous person to interview for this book. He's a real character himself, raising chickens in the Canadian outback, he has the best stories![1]

What made you want to become an animator?

I grew up watching old Warner Brothers and Disney Cartoons. I got into drawing at a very young age and dreamed about working for Disney as an animator. My first job was in a Cinema/Television Studio, there were a lot of talented people working there. For instance, the guy who sat next to me used to work for Disney. He spent 11 years there, animating main characters like "Tarzan" and the Genie in "Aladdin". We became very good friends; I traded Maya knowledge for animation tips from him! This friendship gave me perspective on studios like Disney. The golden years were over, there were massive layoffs and the whole industry started shifting to other medias like 3D animation instead of traditional drawing.

I decided to focus on 3D animation and keep drawing in my free time. Eventually, I moved towards the game industry, hoping that the animation level in games would flourish and increase in quality.

When I look back now I believe I made the right decision.

How did you get your first job as an animator?

I was incredibly persistent. I got my first job in the industry because I would call the same studio relentlessly. They ended up hiring me because they got tired of me calling them . . . Not sure if this is a great idea anymore but it worked for me!

It started with them asking me to send them my demo and resume via mail. Back then, we were recording our demo reels on a VHS tape . . . No YouTube! So, I decided to go and deliver the tape myself, this is when I managed to get the CEO's phone number at the reception. I had to insist . . .

Then, I started calling three to five times a day. At some point, the CEO told me: "I am tired of you calling me, Steve. I am a busy guy; I can't take time to talk to you on the phone anymore. I guess I will have to give you an interview to make you stop calling me . . .".

My English level was very bad, and I had to lie about being an expert in Layout . . . But I got the job. I had one weekend to educate myself on how to become an expert in Layout. I managed to become a layout artist

[1] Fun fact: Steve has two chickens named after Ellise and me!

and, in no time, got promoted to lead! Learning this craft gave me valuable knowledge on composition and cameras.

What's your top tip for someone starting out looking for a job?

Prepare yourself for interviews. When they ask you if you have questions, make sure you seize the opportunity to show how much you know about their studio and the games they've worked on. This proves that you haven't blindly applied to a studio and not bothered to look at what they actually do, it shows you want to work there. As an employer, it always feels better to hire someone that has the desire to work for you.

What skill would you recommend someone to work on in the meantime of finding a job?

For cinema, I recommend life drawing and acting classes. For video games, I recommend game engines like Unreal and Unity.

Make sure you are always busy and that people know that you are. When I got my last job, they ran a background check on my career. There was an error on my LinkedIn between December 2006 and January 2007. There was a month missing there. They actually asked me what I did during that month and if I was jobless. Turns out it was only a mistake related to a job switch.

Now you see how important it is to stay active. . . . If you are looking for a job and can't find one, take a class or get a tutorial to learn something new related to animation.

When they will ask you what you have done, your answer will show your dedication to the craft.

What qualities do you look for when hiring a junior animator?

It all starts with Passion. Someone passionate will work harder than someone talented. Over time, passion will supersede skill. A combination of talent and passion makes incredibly skilled animators.

Is there something you particularly like to see in a person's showreel?

A great walk with some acting in it is my favourite thing to see in a reel. I also love shots that have great timing with audio. It shows that the animator has a notion of what beats are.

Performance pieces with different emotional beats and acting tones, especially if synced with dialogue, can be a really cool way to show your creativity.

And of course, make sure you show some good body mechanics with great weight shifts.

What was the most important lesson you learned in your first year in the industry?

That everyone is replaceable. So, do not only work at your best, be at your best with people too. I have seen scenarios where someone less talented got picked over a better-skilled candidate because that person knew how to work in a team.

I got laid off six weeks after getting hired for my first job . . . My first contract was a six-week try-out. Yes, it was very different back then. I seemed to make a very good impression by being nice to people and proactive. Everyone would say that if the bosses do choose to let me go after six weeks, they would all raid the CEO's office to get me my job back. In my head, that is the kind of thing people say, but never happens. . . .

On that crucial last day, when I got the announcement that I was losing my job, the whole floor moved towards the CEO's office complaining about the situation while I was gathering my belongings.

I ended up being laid off . . . for 15 minutes before getting my job back!

If you were to go back to the beginning of your career, would you do anything differently?

I would take the opportunity to work in other countries. I feel that I missed out on travelling. . . .

In 2003, I had a job offer to work for Weta Digital. I remember still struggling with English back then, so I turned it down. That is my most profound professional regret to this day . . . not only did I pass on the work experience but I grew up reading these books, "Lord of the Rings" became history with the movies.

I passed on this opportunity because it was not convenient to work so far from home and because my partner didn't want to go. But, if I was offered this chance again as a young animator, I would take it.

Have you made any mistakes that would have been avoidable "if you'd only known" that might help others to know?

Letting other people inform me of my worth. The industry is sometimes hostile and competitive, your self-worth should only be dictated by you. Don't let people's opinions drag you down.

When you feel a bit down and face a difficult task, have some clips of your work ready and take a look at what you achieved with those to cheer you up.

It's important to be able to congratulate yourself on the work you have done. This way, you will be self-sufficient and unshakable.

What is the biggest mistake you see in job applications?

The inability to sell yourself. Do not approach employers thinking they are doing you a favour to let you work for them. It's actually the opposite. . . . Good studios understand how valuable their employees are. Make them understand what you can offer them and how ready you are to adapt and learn with them. It's also helpful to insist on the fact that you want to stay, nobody likes to deal with interviews again two months after hiring someone.

What do you think is the most important quality of a game developer?

Adaptability. It's important to stay open to new work methods. These days with Mocap and AI playing a big part in our jobs, it's important to adapt and keep learning.

If you think you've mastered Unreal, then learn Unity. Being versatile is a big plus when you are looking for a job and plan to stay. When it comes to layoffs, studios will always prioritise people with the most skills and knowledge to work well within a smaller team.

How technical do you feel you need to be as an animator?

Over 20 years ago, it was either technical 100% or artistic 100%. Today, I feel that you need to be 50/50 between the two. It's not all about creating a pretty animation, the final result in the engine is the most important.

Showing a playblast in Maya is not important anymore. Playing your animation in Unreal, showing your director and the rest of the team how responsive it is, now that's today's reality.

It is the duty of a gameplay animator to follow up with the designers and make sure that the animations support the gameplay as intended.

Do you have any recommendations for staying up to date with new technology and pipelines? [it can be quite overwhelming]

Be curious, find out what other people are working on, watch tutorials and strive to expand your knowledge not only on animation. Branch your understanding towards design or technical animation. This way, you become a bridge between two departments. You are a key member of the team and without you, communication on the floor fails. That is what I call "job security".

How do you stay on top of your own personal progression?

I try to stay open to constructive feedback, whatever the source is. Do not close yourself off to learning something new.

Study other animator's pipelines and ask them what tools they use. Make sure you are functional without those tools also. You never know when you will have to face either a new project or a new job with more restrictions on tools.

What would be your dream game to work on?

A horror game. So far I've only had a brief opportunity to do this in working on death cinematic animations for "Dead Space 2". I would very much like the taste of building the tension during gameplay and working on a very entertaining boss fight.

My favourite horror games to this day are: "Resident Evil", "Silent Hill" and "Dead Space".

What would you need to do to make you feel you've "made it"?

Ship my own game. I am currently working on a side project . . . I wrote the story, designed the characters and the environment and worked on the game mechanics.

I got a modest subvention for it from the government. I entered phase 2 and plan to get more budget to expand the team.

What does success look like to you?

Waking up happy that it's Monday, and you get to keep working on your shot that you've been planning in your head during the weekend . . .

What do you do when you're having a bad day?

A bad day for an animator means struggling with an animation. Don't give up, this happens less and less as experience goes. You learn how to trust yourself facing those situations and to not panic. Stay cool headed, take a little break. Rest your eyes . . . then give it another try. If you have other assignments, work on something else for a bit.

Do not let people assign your work to someone else. This happened to me twice in over 20 years and I still remember it. Don't give up, you will find a way to deliver the task.

What is the best piece of advice you've received?

Always deliver your work to the best of your knowledge, whatever it is. If you can make a boring animation fun to watch, nothing can stop you.

I remember working at Electronic Arts, I was at intermediate level, and they placed a senior next to me because nobody would sit beside him. He would project negativity in general and one day he looked on my monitor and told me: "This shot you are working on looks fun. They always give me the boring tasks. How come you get to work on those amazing animations . . .".

My assignment was a walk cycle, and he was working on an amazing cinematic shot. I just told him that only his perception towards his work made it boring. I was pretty sure that if we swapped our assignments, he would have said the same thing to me . . .

Always try to be positive and find enjoyment in what you are working on.

Final words?

I still have about 20 good years in this industry, so it's too early for final words . . . :)

Stay Connected, Get Inspired (+ Make Friends!)

16

The internet is a wonderful place. We have all the information, reference, inspiration and cute puppy videos we could think of at the click of a button. This is incredibly useful not only for gathering reference but also for connecting and engaging with potentially invaluable contacts.

16.1 SOCIAL MEDIA

Utilise social media as the powerful tool that it is to help you better understand the industry, what you might expect, characteristics studios look out for and general experiences. You would be surprised at how many people in the industry that would be willing to offer advice and give you feedback, it just takes someone to ask and to ask politely. The worst that can happen is they say no or ignore you but leave it at that.

That being said, the drawback of social media is that we don't fully understand the implications (with being the first generation to properly use it) of how consuming it is. For all its benefits, it's easy to get sucked into the internet and live there, endlessly scrolling with no real escape. It can also get very toxic very fast, always be careful with what you say on the internet and who you say it to.

DOI: 10.1201/9781003344841-16

16.2 MAKE IT POSITIVE

Sure, the internet can be a negative place but it's controllable and *mostly* avoidable.

- *Filter your feed* – it may sound simple but don't follow accounts that don't make you feel good. Sometimes you can feel obliged to follow colleagues, people you meet at networking events, people from school etc. who can pollute your feed with things you don't care about or stir up unnecessary negative feelings. The bottom line is you don't have to follow anyone, you don't have to follow people back, just follow what you want to see! (you can also have a public and a private account).
- *Follow inspiration* – following other animators, other game developers and accounts that involve hobbies and interests outside of your discipline – your feed should inspire you, not annoy you.
- *Animation and game development communities* – you can connect with truly incredible people that you may never meet but can motivate you every day. People from all over the industry post tips, common mistakes, questions, advice and breakdowns of their work – this is an invaluable way to learn. There are also various online communities that form specifically for animators and game developers with the intention to share information, support people at all stages of their careers, aid in finding new work, make connections and generally encourage each other.[1]

16.3 BE KIND . . .

16.3.1 . . . To Yourself

The problem is that you can do all these things with the intention of making your online experience positive and wholesome yet still feel awful. Which brings us to the root of the issue that is ourselves. The internet has made it incredibly easy for us to compare our lives, rating our successes and feeling shame for not experiencing important life events as quickly as others. This perpetuates the idea that everyone around you is leading a seemingly perfect existence but what you see on social media isn't a representation of real life – it's what people *choose* to share. There's no right way to live your life or specific timeline of success you need to keep to. All you can do is try your best, push to be better and only compare yourself to you.

16.3.2 . . . To Other People

The crucial thing we must focus on is that other people's achievements *are not* a reflection of what you don't have and where you should be. Your first response to seeing someone's happiest moment shouldn't be a mean inner monologue of how rubbish you are, or, in some circumstances, built up contempt towards that person purely for being talented. So often really great things are needlessly construed into our own insecurities and jealousy but who does that benefit? We should always choose to celebrate each other and our accomplishments, you're only hurting yourself if you don't.

Interview With . . . Lana Bachynski | Associate Art Director

Lana has the best energy, and she has the most amazing online presence so please go watch her various videos, talks, interviews, tutorials, livestreams, everything! I don't know how she finds the time to do all that she does, but the animation world is truly blessed to have her in it!

What made you want to become an animator?

The shortest, and possibly most honest answer is that I never really wanted to become an animator, it was just a fun thing I liked to do . . . but I DID want to make video games, and it took me much longer than I'd like to admit connecting those dots.

The longer story, if you're curious goes like this: growing up, art was always a constant in my life. My parents met acting on stage, both of my parents are painters, singers, songwriters and so too with all my siblings. While my father also had his life in business, my mom was a director at a local theatre, and so I spent an inordinate amount of time in the theatre, myself. While I also ended up doing a bunch of acting, it couldn't hold a candle to my one true love: the computer. Or more specifically, computer games. We never owned consoles, but I always knew I wanted to be making video games (specifically, I had my sights set on Blizzard since I was eight or nine years old), but I couldn't fathom a path of how to get there. In the city I grew up in, there was a school that let me get a jump-start on my arts education (Victoria School of the Arts, in Edmonton, Canada), and so when I was 15 or so, I was able to try out animating for the first time. We started out with flip books before making our way into some basic tutorials in Cinema 4D, and the whole thing pretty quickly became my favourite hobby. It was like acting, but I also got to hang out on the computer all day. I loved it. I was animating all the time: showing up to school hours early, staying every day a few hours late just to work in the lab . . . BUT I just thought it was some quirky thing I did. Meanwhile, at home, I'd sit there pondering how I could POSSIBLY work in the games industry someday. Fortunately, a few short months before graduation, I had a very perceptive teacher sit me down, point to the various movie and game posters he had up on the lab walls and say, "People get paid to animate these things, you know . . ." and it all finally clicked. (Thanks, Mr D.)

You're an associate art director now, how did that happen? (the path of an animator doesn't have to be linear; I love that!)

I'm honestly still a little surprised by it, myself. It's definitely never a path I thought I would take. "Art Direction", seemed like the kind of role that needed to be held by an illustrator, concept artist . . . someone who I perceive as being more "artistic". Animating is art, but on the spectrum of true animation thespian to technical animator, I lean more towards the technical side, and so that never seemed like it lined up with this career path very well. However, my understanding of what an art director needs to be, has changed a lot since then. Namely, I have found that I can kind of make this out to be what I want it to be. The role I aim to fulfil is not one purely of making sure colours look harmonious or something (though that happens sometimes), but it speaks directly to how art supports and enhances the gameplay. It's not just about how one particular art discipline looks and feels but looking at the project-level problems we have to solve and working together to identify the right kind of tool to solve it.

I am also super passionate about team dynamics which lends well into any leadership role. For me, being an art director isn't just about the craft, but the processes surrounding it: How do we sync up, avoid stepping on each other's toes, communicate beyond art, or make sure our needs are met in a healthy and effective way? I think my colleagues were looking for a leader who cared about showing up with empathy and vulnerability and more importantly, someone who would make sure people knew that it was okay to do the same.

If I were to try and sum up exactly how it happened (as in: the actual attributes I demonstrated to bring this to fruition), I would say that I am an art director now because I am able to maintain an overall sense of the team/project priorities/vision beyond my craft, I am comfortable working in ambiguity, I am willing to fill in the gaps so others can focus on what they are best at, and I had the opportunity and ability to prove all of the above consistently over time.

What qualities do you look for when hiring a junior animator?

There are a few key things I look for when I'm hiring Junior talent.

One – a solid demo reel. Not too short, not too long, with thoughtfully selected pieces. Thoughtful selection includes making sure that there is a somewhat wide variety of pieces; I don't want to see seven different walk cycles. Even if I see two, I would expect that each of them is showcasing a different skill.

Two – personality and authenticity. This is something that should come through in every facet of your submission if you can manage it: cover letter, demo reel and interview. There's a bit of nuance here: I'm not looking for someone who is hamming it up along the way for show, but someone who will have an opinion. I don't want someone who will simply say yes to everything, but I also don't want someone who will go out of their way to be contrarian. I want someone who is excited and confident, but not someone who thinks they already know everything. In short, I want someone who will be themselves, be kind to others and excited to learn and collaborate.

Three – some amount of experience in a collaborative environment. This one is definitely a bonus, and I want to clarify I don't mean on-the-job-getting-paid-for-doing-this experience, but something that shows up on a resume that indicates they have some soft skills: opt-in collaborative student projects, someone else lighting their scene or rigging their work in their reel, being a leader as a part of a club or organisation. Extra bonus points if the activity subjects them to regular feedback. These kinds of things tell me that they won't be surprised by the environment they'll be asked to work in, and there will likely be fewer growing pains for both of us if they should join the team.

If there was one thing you could say to past-you that was just starting out/trying to get their foot in the door, what would it be?

Spend more time letting yourself learn. For the first few years of university, I spent *so* much time alone, heads down in the lab just trying to power through to make a masterpiece. I thought that the way forward was to "get noticed", and I was on a mission to go above and beyond and make something massive and touching that would strike to the heart of anyone who might be able to witness it. And yeah, if I managed to accomplish that it would likely help get my foot in the door. The only problem was I had no perceivable animation chops and/or other skills to actually get the job done.

In the end, I got infinitely better than I ever would have expected the moment I stopped trying so hard to do the biggest, most challenging thing first. If you are just starting out, I urge you to spend the time and find the joy in what can feel like rudimentary assignments (bouncing balls, weight exercises and pendulums) and really think deeply about what each one of those things is trying to get you to learn. And more importantly, don't do it alone; talk to other people! If you aren't sure what the takeaways should be, walk through it with someone else. You'll make a pal, and both be better for it.

What's your top tip for someone starting out looking for a job?

Apply everywhere, not just your "dream job". Not to say you should give up on your dreams, but rather that it's better to be in it, getting experience anywhere instead of waiting months or even years for openings to pop up at a specific studio.

What skill would you recommend someone to work on in the meantime of finding a job?

I know this industry can be volatile – and there are many reasons why someone might be getting turned away from a job – if you're reading this and you've come up against rejection after rejection, I can't recommend anything more than focusing on your craft. Supplemental skills are great for the workplace, but I would never hire an animator for their life drawing skills. I would also never hire someone who learns how to do some game engine implementation stuff if their demo reel is half-baked.

So, while you're waiting around to get the call backs, I recommend getting serious feedback on your reel from someone you trust and then focusing in on those areas with targeted exercises. Not with the sole purpose of adding it to your demo reel, I find that adds too much pressure, but simply for the sake of improvement.

What was the most important lesson you learned in your first year in the industry?

If you think you're communicating enough, you aren't.

Saying something once or twice in a meeting won't get the point across. Telling one other person won't get the message to the rest of the team. Asking only one out of every five questions that pop into your head won't make you seem more professional or wise, and not taking notes won't make you seem like you've got it handled – all the above will only make you more likely to make a critical mistake! Default to over-communicating on every possible vector and you will be better for it.

If you were to go back to the beginning of your career, would you do anything differently?

It's tough to say. There were many circumstances that if I came up against them now, I would certainly react differently than I did then, but with all things considered, I feel very fortunate to have lucked into making a lot of the right choices. Probably the only thing that I *still* struggle with is saying "no" sometimes, or rather, understanding my own limits. I love making games, and so if you give me basically any fork in the road and ask me to pick between X and making games, I pick games every time. Which is cool that I get to do that! But that has come at the cost of my own health, often enough. I've been in the hospital from stress, bad posture, bad habits . . . all of which have been entirely self-imposed. If I were to go back to the beginning, I would actively seek to set boundaries for myself and try to understand what hills are really worth dying on.

Who [or what] has been your biggest inspiration?

I could write a novel about the people who have and continue to inspire me: Careena Kingdom, Tyson Murphy, Cory Barlog, Todd Howard, Mike Jungbluth, Mariel Cartwright . . . each of them has had a distinct impact on me, the way I work, connect and the dreams I have about my career. But when it comes to the "who" there is always one person who jumps to the front of my mind: Eric Henze, my first animation lead.

Eric joined my team during a time where tensions were pretty high. I had only been at the company for a few months, but a few other animators were all vying for the lead position, and it was causing *drama*. Eric came in, a crazy talented animator with a long history of doing awesome things and I was honestly very worried it would only stir up more of the stress; however, he not only diffused any of those tensions but united the animation team; Eric rallied us into something vastly beyond what we ever would have been. He helped us write aspirational project goals and planned with us for how to get there with our limited resources. Eric saw the strengths of all the animators on the team and consistently set each individual up not just to succeed, but to shine. Eric not only guided me through some of the most vulnerable years of my career but also actively fought for me, protected me, celebrated me and gave me all the tools I would need to succeed wherever I might go.

When it comes to my ongoing inspiration, however, I think the biggest thing that continues to drive me is simply my own desire to make fun and give fun to other people. I love making games and I want to do it all. I want to make a bunch of terrible but functional art, and I want to make something immersive and polished. I want to be in endless meetings triaging bugs, and I'd love to own and guide a vision. I want to wrestle a project from start to finish, and then do it all over again.

What is the biggest mistake you see in job applications?

Applying to the same job or company repeatedly with no perceivable change in application materials. I think that when you're applying online it feels a lot like screaming into the void, but we can see it on the other side of the submission form, I promise! When I see a demo reel that previously got rejected get submitted for the second, third, fourth time with no attempt at swapping pieces in or out, I feel like that tells me more about who you are and your craft than I would ever learn in an interview.

What do you think is the most important quality of a game developer?

The most important quality is tough because there are so many ways to bring value to a team, but there are two things I think are pretty evergreen:

Communication and Collaboration: you've gotta be able to play nice with others.

Able to work well in ambiguity: when you're making a brand-new game, there is no instruction manual that comes with the territory. There will be many, many times you will head into a situation where there is no obvious expectation of the desired result. Being able to get into that space, make some initial choices, fail fast and get the answers your team needs to move forward is so, so valuable.

How technical do you feel animators should be?

As technical as you want to be, so long as you are technical enough to get the job done. In many cases that will be just enough to be able to get in and learn to use the DCC of choice (Maya, 3ds Max etc.) and export to the engine. However, every iota of technical skill past that only makes you more valuable on many if not most teams, so it's good to consider more than the baseline investment in your technical prowess.

Do you have any recommendations for staying up to date with new technology and pipelines? [it can be quite overwhelming]

There will always be so much technology emerging it really will be impossible to truly keep up with it all. I would recommend following a tech blog that you like and trust and peeking your head into conferences now and again to see what other folks are doing. BUT the big red-flag-danger I will wave is with proprietary engines. If your company is using proprietary tech, consider putting an equal amount of time learning all the things you learn in the proprietary engine, in something more commonly accessible like Unreal or Godot. I did not do that. It hurts me how much niche technical knowledge I have about something that is valueless in the wider industry. I was one of the most technical animators on my team and after leaving the company, I had absolutely nothing to show for it.

What would you need to do to make you feel you've "made it"?

I try to keep lofty dreams (i.e. Game Direction) because I'm excited about it, but I don't try to hang all of my self-worth on anything in particular. I went to school to be an animator and since then I've been continuously paid to do so. I think the moment that I got my first paycheque I felt like I hit the jackpot. I was in an empty apartment, sleeping on a yoga mat for months, barely had enough money for basic groceries, but you know what: I was doing what I set out to do and that is enough for me.

What does success look like to you?

Honestly: anything that makes you happy and living free of the FOMO. The grass is truly *always* greener: folks working in indie who wish they were up in AAA, folks working in AAA who wish they were being scrappy indie devs. People working in games who wish they could be in film, and people in film wishing they had what we do in games. Living your life, the way that works for you, keeps you balanced and has you celebrating your choices instead of looking over your shoulder to see if you should be doing something else. Happiness and stability (at no cost to anyone else). That feels like success to me.

What do you do when you're having a bad day?

Sometimes I want to mentally check out and just play some games or watch a show. But honestly, the only things that will really snap me out of a funk are taking some time to exercise and talking to someone. When I'm having a bad day, I always feel like I gotta get the poison out. Whether it be a lack of inspiration or confidence, frustration with something about the project, or even just general lethargy . . . I gotta talk it out or I gotta work it out. Maybe sometimes even both.

Working out is great because even on a day where I feel like I accomplished nothing, I can at least say "well I had a nice walk", and then there is something.

Talking is often even better because so much of the time it's just because I'm up in my head. Having to spit words out in a way that is comprehensible to someone else will often organise things for me. It also can build up trust and camaraderie to be vulnerable. Sure, I'm able to see that I'm not alone, but especially in a leadership position, it can be powerful to admit you don't have all the answers – it shows people that *they* are not alone.

What is the best piece of advice you've received?

If you have more than three priorities, then you do not have any at all.

(I don't know if it's the *best*, but certainly one that pops up more often than I'd like to admit.)

Final words?

Ya know, I think I'm fresh out. Thanks, Hollie, for including me and for your patience in me getting these questions back to you!!! <3 <3 <3

NOTE

1 See *Luna's Learning Lab* for suggestions.

Focus on Happiness

17

Sometimes I think we can get caught up in the concept of having a "Passion Job" and by that, I mean we put too much pressure on our jobs defining us. Most of us choose this industry because we are passionate, we want to make a career around something we genuinely enjoy and care about. If we're going to spend our days doing something to earn money, why can't it be something we actually find fun? I think that's the best thing about it, however, it doesn't mean *being an animator* has to be your whole life.

17.1 A JOB IS A JOB (. . . NO MATTER HOW COOL IT IS!)

Believe me when I say that I mean this with all the cliché connotations it usually entails – you only have one life, *live it!* At the end of the day, no matter how much you enjoy your job (and don't get me wrong, enjoying your job means *a lot!*), there is so much more to do in your life than *just* have a career. It's not enough anymore, gone are the days of choosing a career *or* family – have it all and accept nothing less!

17.2 GET RID OF THE GUILT

Stop feeling guilty for not being productive 100% of the time! All you can do is your best in the hours you're paid for, sometimes you'll *want to* stay late to finish something and that's your choice, but you should never feel like you

 DOI: 10.1201/9781003344841-17

need to stay late. Working too many hours is often counterproductive because you'll no doubt be sacrificing other aspects of your life to do it.

Another side of guilt can be thinking you need to be working on personal projects when you come home. Whilst it is a fact that the more practice you get, the better you'll be, it's not worth burning yourself out over. When you come home after being at work all day, you should do whatever makes you happy. If working on stuff at home makes you happy, then power to you! – do it because you *want* to do it, not because you feel you *need* to do it.

17.3 VALUE YOUR TIME

You can't get it back. Spend time with your friends and family, go do things – scary things, silly things, adventurous things and cute things! Staying late at work doesn't amount to much more than you could probably have done in the morning, but it does take important hours from you that you could have spent meeting a friend for an iced coffee or better yet – cuddling your dog! Put value in your life both inside and outside of work, it really matters.

Interview With . . . Christine Phelan | Animator and Wildlife Ecologist

Christine is simply incredible. I was super lucky to have met her at Konsoll, where we were both giving talks, she's one of the most interesting people I've ever met. The couple of days I got to chat to her just wasn't enough so what better excuse than to interview her for my book!

What made you want to become an animator?

Without hesitation, I can say it was Jurassic Park. I saw it in theatres when I was nine years old, and it simultaneously terrified me and blew my mind. I fully believed in those dinosaurs from start to finish, and the difference between what was visually possible prior to that film and the effective use of practical and digital effects in Jurassic Park is a core memory for me. The film suggested that somewhere out there it was not only someone's job to bring dinosaurs to life and make them act and perform how they wanted them to, but that it could be done in an incredibly believable way. I didn't have a word for "creature animator" then, but it certainly set me down that path!

You have a massive interest in wildlife and animals, could you talk a little about that (+ how you balance that side of your life alongside being a super-talented animator!!)

When I was a kid, I was obsessed with video games of all genres and grew up on a raw free-range diet of console games. I was particularly drawn to games where world building, NPC behaviour and character design felt well married to one another. "Metal Gear Solid" is probably the game that nudged me from "I love to play games" to "I want to make games", as it was the first game I'd played that had a very direct (and reality bending) conversation with the player, that was the first time I was really aware of the developers as participants in that conversation.

Simultaneously, I loved science as a kid (earth sciences like geology and oceanography but biology most of all) and have always been fascinated by animal behaviour and how it is expressed through movement. Of course, dinosaurs and fantasy/sci-fi creatures were always rad – they represent a lot of wild ideas and were opportunities to try out unique and interesting designs – but I was most interested in the lives and survival strategies of existing animals that we can observe and study, many of whom lead rich lives we know very little about.

I ravenously consumed anything David Attenborough or Steve Irwin produced, and I had an encyclopaedic recall of any and every animal fact you could imagine (it will come as no surprise that one of my favourite games growing up was "Pokémon"). The interaction between organisms and their environments, or "ecology", was the most interesting part to me – system-wide interactions like predator–prey dynamics, migration patterns stimulated by changes in season or resource availability, or when and how young animals disperse to find their own territory. Animal movement at the individual and landscape scale is what gets my gears turning, and I'm interested in the why of it just as much as the how.

To me, game animation is an artistic expression of those concepts: I am not only responsible for creating the individual character movements but those individual performances are combined as a set to be a creature's behavioural response to a player, other creatures or environmental changes in the level they exist in. These animations can even be the expressions of a player-controlled creature itself.

I've spent nearly 17 years working as an animator and a game developer. I have had the opportunity to work on some really fun, memorable creature animations and deeply rewarding game projects, but I eventually hit a point in my career where many of the projects I was working on wound up getting cancelled or never fully realised. While some cutting of material is just part of the "cost of doing business" in a creative field, this eventually amounted to years of mental and emotional investment that just kind of . . . disappeared overnight. It gave me pause and made me think about what I wanted for the rest of my future, and whether it was time to pursue that other passion – biology – that had always driven the animation work that I loved doing.

So, while continuing to work as a full-time game dev, I went back to school to take science and math courses in order to bridge the gap between my BFA and pursuing graduate studies in wildlife research. I sought opportunities to do practical work in the field which started as small volunteer gigs on the weekends, and eventually grew to bigger roles as I gained more experience. What really unlocked my current trajectory was when I began training in how to interpret wildlife track and sign, which is how we read the clues that animals leave behind (such as footprints in the snow, signs of feeding on a shrub and poop next to a tree) that can tell us something about who it is, where they went and what they did while they were there.

Since then, I've worked on a number of projects that use tracking as the main means of data collection: searching for new-born deer fawns to put radio collars on them, trailing elephants that crop-raid small farms to see where they went, and which plants they eat and avoid, trailing cougars fitted with accelerometer collars to match the motion data captured on the hardware to the footfall patterns they leave behind in the snow, backtracking wolves from a kill-site to where they first encountered their prey to see how and where snow conditions made it impossible for their prey to escape, and, finally, using snow tracking to study how Canada lynx hunt and travel in forests that are regenerating after large-scale wildfires.

Just a few months ago, I finally managed to convince a wildlife researcher that this animator could hack it as a real scientist, and I was accepted into a graduate research program to study wildlife and continue my work with Canada lynx full-time. My passion has always been to work with animal movement – whether it was virtual or literal – and having the opportunity to conduct field research on animal movement at the individual and landscape scale that helps inform wildlife and forest conservation strategies still feels unreal to me.

It's been a long (very long) road to get here, something I could only imagine as a kid and later as an adult, but I couldn't ask for an opportunity that overlapped more with what makes my heart sing, what I am interested to learn about, the ways I want to push myself and grow, and the impact I want to have on the world. The Venn diagram is essentially a circle. I am very excited for this next chapter of my life, but I can't envision a world in which I am no longer an animator and game developer in some capacity. I love that work and creative space too much to leave it behind entirely and, as I am already finding with my graduate studies, there is enormous overlap between the thought processes and creative problem-solving of game dev and scientific research. I think being a researcher can only make me a better game developer, and I can't wait to see where this odd, winding path through life takes me next.

If there was one thing you could say to past-you that was just starting out/trying to get their foot in the door, what would it be?

I would tell her that Christine is never late nor is she early, she arrives precisely when she means to. I had to get comfortable with following a winding path to some of my career goals, but oftentimes taking "the long way" to reach my goals was much more fulfilling, educational and experience-laden than the direct path. I have learned an enormous amount about what I do and don't want (in my career and in my life), by taking opportunities that initially seemed tangential to my long-term goals and developed skills that transcend individual jobs or disciplines. I'm a scientist now, but so much of my experience working as a game developer and an animator are directly transferable (and sometimes my secret weapons!) to my research, and how I solve problems creatively, or communicate complex concepts to broad audiences. I think I've had a richer career and life experience for taking the scenic route, because it's just allowed me to add more tools to my Batman utility belt.

What's your top tip for someone starting out looking for a job?

Be flexible and take smaller, incremental steps towards your goals. Having a waypoint in the distance that drives your overall trajectory (whether it's a studio you want to work for, a personal project you want to do, a specific piece for your reel etc.) is very important and useful, but it is okay if your path to your destination isn't a straight line. Maybe even vital. Breaking a task up into smaller steps will make it easier to get to where you want to go and gives you an opportunity to acknowledge the progress you are making. I've met a number of people who had the "Pixar or bust" attitude that ultimately denied themselves that very opportunity because they wouldn't take the smaller, perhaps less "glamorous" steps that presented themselves as opportunities to learn, grow and develop the skills they needed in order to reach those bigger goals.

If you were to go back to the beginning of your career, would you do anything differently?

Gosh. If I could go back to the beginning of my career, I would work fewer hours and place a higher value (monetary and personal) on my time. At my first game dev job, I was easily working between 80 and 90 hours each week for months on end. While this company no longer exists, this is sadly a widespread expectation and practice across the industry. It is unsustainable and exploitative to allow, encourage and require that kind of work schedule, especially of folks new to the industry, and it is often the result of poor project planning. The time and financial shortfalls become the burden of workers later in the project. Self-advocacy for pay and work-life balance were not taught to me in school, and so they were hard-learned lessons throughout my career only after finding out how I was being exploited or underpaid. You don't get that time back, so it's important to understand that when making those trade-offs.

Who [or what] has been your biggest inspiration?

Who: Dr Stuart Sumida, a palaeontologist and professor of biology at the California State University San Bernardino who flirts with the dark arts of animation. He is an incredibly engaging speaker that delivers fantastic and insightful lectures on morphology-driven motion and has been an animation consultant for several games and films. He's a scientist with the enthusiasm and heart of an animator, and I am inspired by his ability to move between those two worlds with such ease. That fact has played no small part in my life as an animator who flirts with the dark arts of science!

What: I love thinking about animal movement, and quadrupedal movement specifically. It's complex, nuanced and full of learning opportunities! Plantigrade (bears and raccoons), digitigrade (canines and felines) and unguligrade creatures (horses, deer and rhinos) have very different foot structures that affect their base-line movement and locomotion. There is an incredible amount of variety within each category depending on the animal's size, life history and behaviour! Domestic dogs are great teachers as well as tricksters: while you have the same basic body plan across hundreds of different breeds, there is so much variety from one to the next and it forces you to pay attention to what their motion *actually* looks like, and how it differs based on morphology. A Corgi does not move the same as a Great Dane, which does not move the same as an American bulldog, and if you treat them as interchangeable movements and slap the same walk cycle on each of those body types, you're missing the most interesting part of animation!

What do you think is the most important quality of a game developer?

I think the most important quality of a game developer is resilience for when things, invariably, do not go according to plan. Games are all about experimentation and pivoting when your ideas don't work the way you expect them to, and I have never met a game design document that withstood the test of time and development from start to finish. Being able to respond to player feedback at any level in the process (from individual animation through to full gameplay/level design) and draw from that feedback in a productive and creative way is, to me, the hallmark of a great game developer. Some of our best features or moments in "Half-Life: Alyx came" from observing player behaviour and incorporating unexpected responses to what we'd made directly into our game design.

How technical do you feel animators should be?

I think it is always to an animator's benefit to be technically inclined, or at least technology curious. It not only expands our ability to create compelling, detailed, nuanced performances in a gameplay context (when working with animation state graphs!), it also makes us independent creators, and more able to experiment and implement our own ideas. The more technical you are, the more you can create and the more direct control you can have over your work further through the implementation and development process. With animation state machines, I just think of it as another animation pass that I need to do in order to take something from concept to completion.

What would be your dream game to work on?

I am very privileged to be able to say that I've gotten to work on them, really. "Brütal Legend and Half-Life: Alyx" were very different products but were immensely fulfilling to work on, creatively and intellectually. VR games and experiences are difficult to do well, but create some spectacular lived experiences, and to be able to create a memory for someone in that context is incredibly powerful. Getting to touch "Team Fortress 2", even for a little bit, was another career goal of mine that I am so glad to have reached.

I have a few wildlife-related game concepts rattling around in my head, but they are for another day and definitely after my graduate studies. I have wildlife research that I need to finish first!

What would you need to do to make you feel you've "made it"?

I think the expected answer might be the financial success of a product or how widely it's been played. While both of those certainly feel nice, they are usually so far outside of my direct influence, unless it is something I have produced with a really small group or on my own and I can really see my fingerprints on. The biggest things for me are (1) do players notice and genuinely enjoy the work that I have done and (2) "Was the experience, collaborating with the people I made this with, a good one?" There are a couple of technical artists, level designers, and gameplay programmers who I would happily make absolute trash with because we work together so well. As I've progressed in my career, working on cool titles has taken a back seat relative to finding those collaborative partnerships as a gameplay animator. They can be rare if you're on a larger team that keeps disciplines from interacting too much, but it's incredibly fulfilling when you do.

What does success look like to you?

My personal measure of success is getting people to laugh, or making them want to barf, with animation I've made. Eliciting a visceral, lizard-brain response from a player or a viewer is really rewarding because it's an honest reaction. My second measure of success is if I make myself laugh or want to barf with my animation.

What do you do when you're having a bad day?

I am fortunate enough to live in a mountainous part of the United States, and when I am having a particularly rough go of it, I need to put miles of trail under my boots. The steeper the grade and more miserable the slog, the better. Hiking a lung-buster requires so much of my mental attention to focus on what I am doing right in that moment that whatever gunk I am churning through in my life gets banished to the backburner, where my brain can run through it subconsciously. I inevitably emerge feeling better, yet exhausted, but that bit of mental distance from whatever I've been dealing with enables me to be able to think more clearly.

What is the best piece of advice you've received?

"You have one thousand awful drawings you need to get out of your system before you do your first good one, so you'd better get started". This very blunt advice is applicable to many aspects of life, not just animation. Developing a new skill takes time, practice and most importantly numerous mistakes and failed attempts. Failure is such a healthy part of learning and is only a negative if we do not learn from the experience. Doing something and then understanding afterwards why it needs to be done differently is the hallmark of learning and growth. It's critical to the whole process.

Final words?

Animation is an exciting, fulfilling, even magical skill to develop and can be immensely rewarding because you are, if you're lucky, genuinely breathing a spark of life into a character. The work you do allows them to exist, to think, to feel apart from you. A well-animated character can be utterly believable on its own, and there's really nothing like it.

Preceding the final product, however, is a period in the development of every animation that I think of as "the ugly stage". It's brutal. You start off well, you're laying down your key poses, exploring the broad strokes of posing and timing and rhythm, and you're cruising through frames in what feels like no time at all. It's great! You're enthusiastic, you're absolutely crushing it!

Then you hit a snag. One of the actions you've started building is perhaps a little more complex than you originally thought and if you weren't keeping a close eye on the graph editor, it doesn't resolve cleanly, and you need to rebuild parts of it. Or maybe you got all your keyframes knocked out with stepped curves and after switching it over to splines to start refining it, all of the energy feels like it's just . . . evaporated. Everything you built is still there, structurally the animation is perfectly sound, but now it somehow feels duller, lacking in crispness or like there's something missing.

Congratulations, you've just arrived at the hardest part of an animation. This is where every increment of progress feels further from the next and pose or curve adjustments can be fraught with peril because what you've sketched out has evolved into something more complex and intertwined with itself, and you need to be careful about where and how you make your changes.

The ugly stage is something every animator, no matter their raw talent or experience level, endures. It will be hard work and there won't always be a clear solution *but* if you can endure the difficulties of the process (in animation, and in life) what you're left with is something that has the capacity to be entertaining, beautiful and truly alive.

The Reality of Game Development

18

There's a very common misconception that working in the games industry means you *just play games all day*. Of course, that's far from the truth, which I hope has come across by this point in the book! It's often the case that people entering this industry assume it will be this fairy-tale job, that nothing ever goes wrong, people don't disagree with each other, the game will always ship and be successful. Ultimately it will get stressful at times, you won't agree with every decision, projects get cancelled, people leave – it's important to acknowledge that these things can and do happen but it's equally as important to keep in mind that these things are miniscule in comparison to all the amazing things that happen, all the fun days, the wins and the sense of pride you get for yourself and your team's achievements.

18.1 NOT ALL STUDIOS WORK ON THEIR OWN GAMES

Every game studio is made up a little differently and this influences the kinds of projects that a studio will work on. This is something to think about when choosing the studio you want to work for as there are lots of different *types* of projects that have nothing to do with subject matter.

- *Original IP* – a studio has come up with its own idea for a game completely independently, giving them full creative control. Unless this game is self-published, it would need to be sold to a publisher which risks full freedom of decision-making.

DOI: 10.1201/9781003344841-18

- *Third-party IP* – a publisher has gone to a studio with an idea and pays them to make it. How much say that studio has over the game varies but has the potential to feel very similar to an original.
- *Co-development* – a studio works with another studio to help them ship their game. The outlook the primary studio adopts towards their co-dev partnerships greatly influences the ownership and creative freedom the partner has. The involvement, input and enthusiasm another studio can have in these scenarios is hypothetically huge, *if* the primary studio allows and nurtures that type of ownership.
- *Outsource* – a studio creates assets for another studio's game with little to no input on the work they produce, largely in isolation to the project.

An indicator of the potential projects a studio will likely be working on is usually evident in the previous projects that studio has shipped, more often than not studios will work on projects they have proven talent and expertise on. I know that sounds obvious, but it wasn't something I considered when applying for jobs – studios have their own identities. Consider this when figuring out which studio is the right fit for you, research what you can and ask questions in your interviews to better understand the types of projects you'll likely be working on.

18.2 YOU'LL WORK ON GAMES YOU WOULDN'T PLAY YOURSELF

This might not matter to you but it's worth noting that you're not always going to like the games you work on. It's not always going to be your favoured subject matter, style or genre but that doesn't mean you won't enjoy developing it, nonetheless. Learning to adapt your knowledge base and skill set to things you don't fully understand is a staple quality of being a distinguished game developer and it's a great opportunity to step out of your comfort zone. I don't think any of us chose this path because we thought it would be easy . . .

18.3 THE INPUT YOU HAVE WILL VARY

As soon as you care about something you naturally become invested and with this comes unnecessary frustration and even resentment when things don't go how you expected. The vital thing to do in this situation is to take a step back and accept what you *can* control and what you *can't*. There are many things that simply *happen* for instance *when* you come onto a project – midway or towards the end can be very tough as you are at the mercy of whatever has already been set up with little room for adaptation or adjustment. The *type* of project will affect your input too, luckily a lot of studios steer away from outsourcing and put more focus on co-development which *should* encourage some form of ownership. All your effort should be put into you and your department, ensuring you do your bit well is all you should worry about. Take advantage of situations where you can offer your opinions constructively – playtests, team/ feature meetings and reviews.

18.4 IT DOESN'T ALWAYS WORK OUT

Ultimately, we cannot singlehandedly control the success of a game, even a perfectly developed game can fail simply due to timing. One of the most important things you must remember is to *separate the game's success from your own*. There are a million reasons a game can fail that have absolutely nothing to do with the job you did, it's ridiculous to dismiss your achievements simply for the luck of the draw. Something game developers can understand, that the mean trolls of the internet do not, is the four years and more of development it takes to make a game. Years of lessons, mistakes, funny stories, tears, laughter, problems solved, cool things you never knew were possible – achieved, honestly the public opinion of the game is a small part of what you should accredit your accomplishments to. Work to make *yourself* proud.

Closing Thoughts

19

If you're reading this you've made it to the end, thank you! I'm super grateful you've taken the time to read this book, this is essentially everything I've learned so far. Even whilst writing this book I've experienced more and tried to add stuff as I live it! I hope you feel at least slightly better and if you feel even the tiniest bit more confident and appreciative of yourself – I'll be very happy for it.

19.1 CELEBRATE YOURSELF

You did it! You graduated! You got a job! You made friends! You survived your first day, month, year, meeting, playtest, lunch, review! There are so many new experiences, things that past-you would have been terrified at the thought of, that you have completely nailed. Take time to celebrate yourself for everything you've accomplished, you worked really hard for all of this, and you deserve all of it. Now you've come this far just think about how far you have yet to go!

19.2 PAY IT FORWARD

Treat others the way you want to be treated. Remember how it feels to be the new person and try to be as welcoming as you can to the newbies. It's daunting for anyone to start at a new company whether that be their first ever company

   DOI: 10.1201/9781003344841-19

or their seventh, as simple of a gesture as asking a person if they want to come for lunch can go a long way.

19.3 STOP WISHING YOUR LIFE AWAY!

Why are we always in a rush? We're always racing ahead to the next milestone without stopping to enjoy the one we're currently in. When I first started, I longed to be one of those insanely talented veterans with 20+ years of experience, someone that knew what they were doing, that wasn't constantly worried they were rubbish! It's funny because the more I've gotten to talking to the people who I thought had it all together, it turns out they're just making it up as they go along too. What I realised, in wishing for that, is that I was essentially wishing 20 years of my life away! When you think about it like that you realise how ridiculous those thoughts really are, of course you can't compare yourself to the talents of those veterans when you first start out but that's just facts – *there is no comparison* so stop comparing!

There's so much we can do with that in-between, why would we want to skip to the end? Enjoy the journey, enjoy animating and enjoy time *not* animating because there will always be a new destination.

19.4 FORGET ABOUT PERFECT

There is no such thing as perfection, there's no perfect path your career must follow, there's no perfect way to animate – there are lots of different ways to do anything and your way is all yours. Be confident with your ideas, be passionate about what you create, fight for what you believe in and don't be scared to be proven wrong.

Don't let your insecurities hold you back, if you've had a cool thought just say it. Embrace curiosity, as much as I apologise for asking silly questions there really is no such thing and I always benefit from asking them! I think all too often we get caught in the trap of assuming someone has already thought that, asked that, done that when in reality everyone might be assuming the same thing. There's no harm in saying something that's already been said but we all lose when nothing gets said.

19.5 FIND YOUR VOICE

Something I struggled with early on in my career was figuring out how much of myself to bring into the workplace. I thought people might not take me as seriously if I came across very *girly*, openly loving unicorns and glitter etc. . . . I entertained the idea of having a more serious persona at work, not talking about myself or my life, not wearing bright colours or being as chatty as I very much am. The problem I had with that is that *wasn't me* and that would take *so* much effort. Something I've come to realise is embracing my personality has really helped me in so many ways. We all learn very similar lessons and face very similar challenges. Translating these situations into your own words painted by your own experiences is what will set you apart from just repeating things you've heard and read. I never thought I'd enjoy public speaking as much as I do now and I think a lot of that comes down to writing presentations exactly how I'd say them, not putting pressure on myself to come across in any particular way or say big words I would never use. I've found that not only is this method far easier to remember but it also comes across way more natural and authentic. Embracing myself and the way I want to do things has funda-mentally changed my perspective on what *being professional* really means.

So, let's not pretend we're all the same person and that the workplace has to be any specific way. Everyone has their own ways of doing things, of speaking, of thinking and it's those differences that can make a team great. My point being, if anyone respects you any less because of the way you dress or for liking pumpkin spice lattes – they're the problem not you.

19.6 WHAT NEXT?

Progression is at the forefront of most people's minds wherever they are in their careers. When will I get that next title? That next pay rise? What can I do to progress? The simple answer is do good work. As I said before, there's no rush to climb the ladder and there's no hidden path to get what you want without putting the work in. Work hard, be proud of the work you produce, absorb as much as you can and be an active participant within your team. Knowledge isn't power, share what you know and listen when people share with you.

The best piece of advice I received in my first year or so in the industry was to "flip the switch" and acknowledge my own worth, it's not arrogant to have confidence in yourself. I would constantly belittle myself as a disclaimer to all the work I did and the only person that hurt was me. There's a line of course and having a massive ego is bad but you're nowhere near that line in saying "Yes, I can do that", and truly believing you can.

19.7 FINALFINALWORDS_02

Please just have as much fun as you can with everything you do, I really believe it shows when people *care,* not only in the work they produce but in the atmosphere they create – they're the people I want to make games with.

Glossary

AAA/AA: games with large to medium budgets

ABP (Animation Blueprint): visual scripts that are used for the creation and control of complex animation behaviours

Additives: adds to the base layer animation

ADR (Animation-Driven Ragdoll): procedural, physical-based animation

AI: Artificial Intelligence

Animation graph: where you create animation-specific logic for your character

Animation notifies: create repeatable events synchronised to animation sequences

ASCII/binary: file types in Maya – binary is not readable, ASCII is readable

Attributes: a position associated with a node that can hold a value or a connection to another node

Bake animation/export: committing animation to the skeleton and saving

Blender: 3D Content Creation Software

BlendShapes: a way of deforming geometry to create a specific look

Blendspace: graphs where you can plot any number of animations to be blended between based on the values of multiple inputs

Blueprint: a high level, visual scripting system that provides an intuitive, node-based interface

Bones: visual cues that illustrate the relationships between joints

Boss Fight: a significant enemy type the player must defeat

Branches: create a copy of the source files and folders that is linked to the source by integration history original

Bugs: an unexpected result that requires a fix

Build: the latest version of the game

Butterworth: removes noise from data without affecting the curve's minimum or maximum values

C++: general-purpose programming language

Camera: defines the way in which we present a view of the game world to the player

Capsule: the collision capsule used as root element of a Pawn or Character

Changelist: a list of files, their revision numbers and operations to be performed on these files.

Channel Box: used to change values, set keys, lock, unlock and create expressions on attributes

Check files in: put your edited files in the depot as the most recent revisions

Check files out: get the latest version from the depot for editing

Cloth dynamics: simulating cloth within a computer program

COG/COM (centre of gravity/centre of mass): the central control of a character

Compliance: ensuring that the game adheres to the platform manufacturers' rules and regulations

Constraints: connections that limit the movement, rotation or scaling of an object based on the position, orientation or size of another object

Control rig: a series of controllers that are linked to the joints of a character's skeleton, allowing you to manipulate a character's pose

Controller: animatable curve or surface that drives the skeleton without keying the data

Craft: skill or experience

Crunch: working significant overtime to deliver a game on schedule

Curves (commonly associated with tangents): defines how an animation is interpolated

Cycle/loop: the first and last frame are the same, the action can play continuously

DCC (digital content creation): 3D software such as Maya, MotionBuilder Blender

Deadline: the latest time or date by which something should be completed

Depot: containers for files

Depth of field: the effect in which objects within some range of distances in a scene appear in focus, and objects nearer or farther than this range appear out of focus

Dev/development/developer: the act of making games

Diff: compare a file with a previous revision to see what's changed

Engine: a comprehensive set of tools to help you build a game from scratch

Euler filter: used to unscramble rotation curves in Maya

Events: created to execute a task or a set of tasks on the occurrence of a specified event

FBIK (full body inverse kinematics): a technique that allows you to create reactive, dynamic characters in Unreal Engine using a Position Based IK framework

FBX: 3D asset exchange format that facilitates higher-fidelity data exchange between Maya, MotionBuilder and other propriety and third-party software

Feature: a broad term to refer to a large body of work

First person: player assumes field of vision of the character

FK (forward kinematics): calculates the position and orientation of an object based on its parent–child hierarchy

Focal length: the distance from the lens to the principal focus

FPS (frames per second): a measure of how many still images, or frames, are displayed in a single second

Frame: a singular image that makes up a sequence of images

FTP (free to play): games that are free to play or don't require payment to continue playing

GaaS (Games as a Service): monetising games after their initial sale

GAS (game ability system): a framework for building attributes, abilities and interactions that an actor can own and trigger

Geometry: 3D mesh

Getting latest: transfers most current version of files to your workspace

Hierarchy: the grouping of child nodes under parent nodes

HS (horizontal slice): indicates the bare minimum needed to have the game playable

Hybrid: flexible working where employees spend some of their time working remotely and some in the office

IK (inverse kinematics): used to connect game characters physically to the world

In-between: the frames between extremes

Indie: independently owned

Integration: to combine changes from one place into another

Interpolate: a process of determining the unknown values that lie in between the known data points

Jira: planning and bug tracking tool that allows developers to understand the status of the project

Joints: the building blocks of skeletons and their points of articulation

Keyframe: defines the start and end of an action and/or the act of animating by hand

KMB: Kinetic Mood Board, a series of moving pictures (gifs/videos) on a singular page that denote a mood or style

Legacy: software, hardware or methodology that has been superseded but is difficult to replace because of its wide use

Local space: position of an object in relation to another object, the origin is the centre of its parent

Locators: small icon like an x–y–z axis that marks a point in space

Locomotion set: typically consisting of an idle, walk/jog/run/sprint loop, directional starts and stop(s)

LOD (level of detail): helps reduce the amount of detail by simplifying polygons and textures as they get further away from the camera

Main: the foundation for development and release streams

Mask: definitions you can add to your skeleton where you can define weight influences, disabling animation from playing partially or fully on specific bones

Mastering/going gold: version of the game is determined good enough to be shipped to stores

Maya: 3D content creation software

Mechanic: a rule or a system that defines how a player can interact with the game and how the game responds to the player's actions

MEL (Maya-Embedded Language): scripting language in Maya

Merging: merges a set of changes from source to target files

Milestones: used to measure the progress of a game project, and to ensure that it meets the expectations and requirements of the developers and publishers

Mobu/MotionBuilder: 3D content creation software

Mocap/motion-capture: recording the motion of people or creatures to then use that data to create animations

Moframe: a phrase used for keyframing motion capture data .

NPC: non-player character

Optimisation: ensures that the gameplay and visual experience are steady no matter what platform it is played on

Outliner: shows a hierarchical list of all objects in the scene in outline form

Overrides: overrides the base-layer animation

Patch: updates post-launch

Perforce: version control that manages source files

Pipeline: a system consisting of people, hardware and software aligned to work in a specific sequential order to do pre-determined tasks in a pre-determined time frame

Placeholder animation: a rough proof of concept to get across an idea/feel, to be replaced with more suitable data

Prototype: the simplest possible execution of a design concept

Python: object-oriented language

QA: quality assurance

Quaternion: a method of rotation that uses a unit quaternion (a quaternion of length one) to represent an orientation in three dimensions

RAW: unprocessed data

Reference: a guide to create a certain look and feel

Remote: working in a location that isn't in the office

Render: the process of computing an image from contents of a scene

Revert: discard changes you've made to your local copy of a depot file

Root marker: the controller that drives the root bone, independent of the character

Root motion: the motion of a character that is based off animation from the root bone of the skeleton

RPG: role-playing games

Shelf/shelving/unshelving: the process of temporarily storing work in progress in the Perforce versioning service without submitting a changelist

Shipping: when a game is finished and launched to the wider public

Showreel: short video containing examples of work that showcase a specified craft

SK (skeletal mesh): type of actor that is used to display complex animation data that was created in an external 3D animation program

Skeleton: a series of joints and bones that form joint chains which you can then pose and animate

Slack: messaging app that connects people to information and other employees

Source control: allows a team to work on the same project from a central repository

Spaces: different coordinate systems

Spline: a tangent commonly used in Maya

Sprints: short and agile way of working on specific tasks or features

Stakeholders: people with a vested interest or stake in the decision-making process

State machine: modular systems you can build in Animation Blueprints in order to define certain animations that can play, and when they are allowed to play

Streams: manage the development and release of files

Submit/create changelist: displays a dialogue where you enter a description of the change and, optionally, delete files from the list of files to be checked in

Tags: conceptual, hierarchical labels with user-defined names

Tangent *(Auto, Spline, Linear, Flat, Clamped, Stepped, Fixed, Plateau)*: the entry and exit of curve segments from a key

The three C's: character, controls and camera – defining factors of the player experience

Third person: you can see the playable character in front of you

Topology: where and how all the edges and vertices are placed to create the mesh surface

Trajectory: a path that an object follows as it moves through space and time, usually under the influence of gravity and other forces

Trigger: used to cause an event to occur when they are interacted with by some other object in the level

UGS *(Unreal Game Sync)*: developer tool that enables them to sync their workspace with an Unreal Project stream

UI: user interface

Unity: game engine

Unreal engine: game engine

UX: user experience

VFX: visual effects

Visual scripting: uses graphical elements, which represent functions, operators or variables

VS (vertical slice): a fully playable portion of a game that shows its developer's intended player experience

Workflow: a series of steps and the discipline to follow them that helps mitigate potential problems

Workspaces: defines the portion of the depot that can be accessed from that workspace and specifies where local copies of files in the depot are stored

World space: position of an object in the overall space, the origin is the centre of the scene

Luna's Learning Lab

A selection of resources to use as a jumping off point for your research.

BOOKS

- **The Animator's Survival Kit** *by Richard Williams*
- **Disney Animation: The Illusion of Life** *by Frank Thomas and Ollie Johnston*
- **Cartoon Animation** *by Preston Blair*
- **Acting for Animators** *by Ed Hooks*
- **Drawn to Life: 20 Golden Years of Disney Master Classes** *by Walt Stanchfield*
- **Game Anim: Video Game Animation Explained** *by Jonathan Cooper*
- **Technical Animation in Video Games** *by Matthew Lake*

COMMUNITIES + BLOGS

---

11 Second Club https://www.11secondclub.com/
AnimState https://www.animstate.com/
The RATanimators https://twitter.com/RATanimators
Tea Time Animation https://www.teatimeanimation.com/
Agora https://agora.community/
Animated Spirit https://www.animatedspirit.com/

EVENTS

GDC (Game Developers Conference)
AnimX
Animex
Konsoll
Unreal Fest
Lightbox Expo
SIGGRAPH (Special Interest Group on Computer Graphics and Interactive Techniques)

TECHNOLOGY

Unreal Engine https://www.unrealengine.com/
Unity https://unity.com/
Blender https://www.blender.org/

MEDIA

Autodesk Tutorials
https://www.youtube.com/@Autodesk_Maya
https://www.youtube.com/@GameDevAcademy
https://www.youtube.com/@mocappys
https://www.youtube.com/@JoCoAnim
https://www.youtube.com/@DustinNelson

Game Technology
https://www.youtube.com/@DigitalFoundry
https://www.youtube.com/@NoclipDocs

Game Dev Perspectives, Interviews, Tutorials
https://www.youtube.com/@harveynewman
https://www.youtube.com/@jeandenishaas
https://www.youtube.com/@KristjanZadziuk
https://www.youtube.com/@gwenfreytheta9649

Guides for Unreal Engine
https://www.youtube.com/@MattLakeTA
https://www.youtube.com/@PrismaticaDev
https://www.youtube.com/@xtruder3D
https://www.youtube.com/@MattAspland
https://www.youtube.com/@reubs

Reference + Inspiration
https://www.youtube.com/@TheCGBros
https://www.youtube.com/@MotionActorInc
https://www.youtube.com/@AaronBlaiseArt
https://www.youtube.com/@Animist_1
https://www.youtube.com/@kevinbparry

Printed in the United States
by Baker & Taylor Publisher Services